101 More Life Skills Games
for Children

SmartFun Books from Hunter House

101 Music Games for Children by Jerry Storms

101 More Music Games for Children by Jerry Storms

101 Dance Games for Children by Paul Rooyackers

101 More Dance Games for Children by Paul Rooyackers

101 Drama Games for Children by Paul Rooyackers

101 More Drama Games for Children by Paul Rooyackers

101 Movement Games for Children by Huberta Wiertsema

101 Language Games for Children by Paul Rooyackers

101 Improv Games for Children and Adults by Bob Bedore

Yoga Games for Children by Danielle Bersma and Marjoke Visscher

The Yoga Adventure for Children by Helen Purperhart

101 Life Skills Games for Children by Bernie Badegruber

101 More Life Skills Games for Children by Bernie Badegruber

101 Cool Pool Games for Children by Kim Rodomista

101 Family Vacation Games by Shando Varda

404 Deskside Activities for Energetic Kids by Barbara Davis, MS, MFA

101 Relaxation Games for Children by Allison Bartl

101 Quick-Thinking Games + Riddles for Children by Allison Bartl

101 Pep-Up Games for Children by Allison Bartl

The Yoga Zoo Adventure by Helen Purperhart

1o1 More Life Skills Games Children

Learning, Growing, Getting Along
(Ages 9 to 15)

Bernie Badegruber

A Hunter House SmartFun Book

Library of Congress Cataloging-in-Publication Data

Badegruber, Bernd.
[Spiele zum Problemlösen. Band 2. English]
101 more life skills games for children : learning, growing, getting along (ages 9 to 15) / Bernie Badegruber.
p. cm.
Summary: "A resource that can help children understand and deal with problems that arise in daily interactions with other children and adults. These games help children develop social and emotional skills and enhance self-awareness"—Provided by publisher.
Includes index.
ISBN-13: 978-0-89793-443-5 (pbk.)
ISBN-10: 0-89793-443-1 (pbk.)
ISBN-13: 978-0-89793-444-2 (spiral bound)
ISBN-10: 0-89793-444-X (spiral bound)
1. Social skills—Study and teaching—Activity programs. 2. Life skills—Study and teaching—Activity programs. 3. Educational games. I. Title: One hundred one more life skills games for children. II. Title: One hundred and one more life skills games for children. III. Title.
LB1139.S6B3213 2005   302'.14'071—dc22   2005015574

Project Credits

Cover Design: Jil Weil & Stefanie Gold
Illustrations: Alois Jesner – Graphikdesign
Book Production: Stefanie Gold
Translator: Elisabeth Wohofsky
Copy Editor: Peter Schneider
Proofreader: Herman Leung
Acquisitions Editor: Jeanne Brondino

Editor: Alexandra Mummery
Customer Service Manager:
  Christina Sverdrup
Order Fulfillment: Washul Lakdhon
Administrator: Theresa Nelson
Computer Support: Peter Eichelberger
Publisher: Kiran S. Rana

Printed and Bound by Bang Printing, Brainerd, Minnesota

Manufactured in the United States of America

9 8 7 6 5 4 3 2   First Edition   08 09 10 11 12

Contents

Adding More Imagination

A detailed list of the games indicating appropriate
group sizes begins on the next page.

Index of Games

Perceiving You

Working with You

We Games

Warming-up Games for the Group

Cooperation Games

Integration Games

Relationship Games

Aggression Games

Preface

What, really, are life skills? Aside from the practical skills required for getting on in life, children need to develop social and emotional skills in order to become well-adjusted adults. These skills are the focus of this book.

In particular, the games in this book and in *101 Life Skills Games for Children* (for children aged 6–12) are designed to foster competence and awareness in the following areas: self-awareness, self-regulation of emotions, active listening, verbal and nonverbal communication, collaboration with others in pairs and larger groups, and observing and understanding other people's feelings. These are essential skills, the building blocks of a successful life. Participating in the games in this book in class or at a camp will help a child to develop at an early age.

We considered calling these areas of social and emotional development life *values* rather than life skills but didn't want to mislead readers into assuming that we are recommending moral principles or prescribing what is right and wrong. Rather, the focus is on developing the foundation skills of self-awareness and getting along with others. Once these foundations are in place, children are better equipped to learn the skills required to become independent. These practical skills are addressed in other books and are likely to be of more value when your children are a little older.

School counselors and teachers have noted an increase in the number of children who have difficulties assimilating into the classroom environment. To help these children, counselors have to rely on strong participation from parents, teachers, educators, and other adults. This book has been created to help them.

Children who have problems in the classroom have a tendency to cause problems for others, too. These children need models for developing social and problem-solving skills. In a structured group they can experience and try out social behavior. They can learn through daily practice and contact with other children. Make-believe situations can help—in make-believe children can find security. With the games in this book, while having fun, children can deal with a current conflict in the classroom or with a make-believe problem that will help prepare them for real-life situations in the future.

Life skills games can also work at the group level, so that group members can develop problem-solving competence as a group and learn to face future problems with confidence. A child who feels safe in a strong group will also be better at facing problems outside the group.

The games in this book are arranged in four sections, according to the ways in which they achieve their goals.

In *I Games,* the communication is mostly one-way. The main skill targeted here is for children to explore themselves and express what they observe. Of course, the children listen to what others have to say, but there is no group reflection about what has been said: no questions asked, no comments made.

You Games focus on how children perceive a partner. They try to learn more about the partner through observation, questioning, responding, commenting, and mirroring. Doing this, they learn a bit more about themselves but also get closer to another person, and then to more and more members of the group.

We Games emphasize the goals of learning to orient oneself in a group, knowing one's position within the group, and recognizing and using the strengths and weaknesses of group members and of the group itself. Children might also learn that a group changes, i.e., that the characteristics of a group fluctuate. Positions, relationships, moods, and potential in a group are partially stable, partially dependent on the situation.

In *We Games,* members of a group learn to recognize differences between their own and other groups, and how to assess and accept other groups.

As the children get better at the earlier games in the book, the group leader can introduce them to the games in the fourth section, *Adding More Imagination.* These games have fewer rules and allow for more creativity.

In each of the four sections, many of the games have "Reflections" and "Role Play" suggestions. The Reflections are examples of questions the leader can ask the children in order to maximize the possibilities for learning and discussion opened up by the games. The Role Play suggestions add another dimension to the games by enabling the players to encounter each other "in character."

We have alternated the use of male and female pronouns throughout the book. Of course, every "he" could be a "she," and every "her" could just as easily be "his."

Introduction

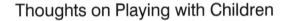

Thoughts on Playing with Children

What Makes an Activity "Play"?

Any activity that is engaged in for its own sake—or just because it's fun—is considered play. Play is about the joy of doing something. In play, earning a living and struggling for survival take a back seat—in fact, results of any kind are of only minor importance. Another characteristic of play is that a game may have an almost infinite number of variations; no one minds if the rules of a game are changed—as long as everyone agrees to it! Variations offer children ways to experiment, to try new experiences and to learn to cope with their environment. Of course, there always needs to be a balance between experimenting and following the rules. This book tries to maintain that balance.

From these thoughts about play, I have derived the following five characteristics that a game should have in order to qualify as play.

The Five Characteristics of Play

1. It doesn't have a clear purpose that children are aware of
If a child doesn't realize that he is supposed to learn something from an activity, the activity is play. Concepts like "learning games" and "playful work" exist only in the adult mind. By controlling the goal, an adult can turn a child's game into "work" without the child realizing it. That is, the adult knows that the child learns from playing (that the play has a purpose), but the child doesn't have to worry about it.

2. It must be voluntary
Play is voluntary. You can stop whenever you want. Nobody can be forced to play a game. The other players may look down on somebody who doesn't want to participate or who quits, but that's all. A teacher or group leader should never force anyone to play a game!

3. The rules are flexible
In an individual or group game, the rules can be changed any time as long

as the new rules are understood by all. Changing, adapting, or even inventing new rules fosters intelligence and creativity.

4. It evokes emotional responses that are short-lived
By emotional responses, I mean intense feelings of joy, expectation, hope, anger, fear, relief, uncertainty, happiness, a sense of belonging, aggression, and so on. On the one hand, these feelings can be intense; on the other hand, they can be defused by remembering "It's just a game." This is a way of learning to deal with tensions constructively. Indeed, if an activity has no tension built into it, a child might not even consider it to be a game—it might feel more like an exercise or merely an activity.

Some of the games in this book can be used as life skills exercises rather than life skills games. This form of social learning is also meaningful but it isn't play, and the leader must be aware of the difference.

5. It benefits from experimentation
A game is perhaps more of a game when there are several ways to play it. There can be different play tactics, goals, and rule interpretations. Experimenting is an opportunity to learn something new. Games that contain multiple possibilities for experimenting, inventing, and creativity are "learning games" in the best possible sense.

Goals of Games

For more information on any of the psychological theories behind how certain goals are achieved in these games, consult the psychologists listed in parentheses below:

Experimenting and experiencing of functions (Jean Piaget)
Practicing and automating (Jean Piaget, G. Stanley Hall, Kar Groos)
Learning and practicing rules (Jean Piaget)
Dealing with drives (G. Stanley Hall)
Experiencing and exerting power (Alfred Adler)
Catharsis (purification) (Sigmund Freud)
Cognitive learning (Jean Piaget)
Activation (Heinz Heckhausen)
Conserving excess energy (Herbert Spencer)

Play Therapy and Game Pedagogy

The purpose of this book is to offer educators a group of games that help them in their work with children. For the children, the games are a way to have fun. For the group leader, they are something more: a way to help children to understand and learn to cope in a game setting with conflicts and problems that might become all too real in the future. It is *not* the job of the game leader to deal with problems and conflicts from a child's past—that task should be left to a therapist. However, the fact that this book doesn't have a primarily therapeutic purpose doesn't mean that it can't be used by therapists in their work.

The following quote paraphrases the Swiss psychologist Hans Zullinger (H. Glotze and W. Jaede, *Die nicht-direktive Spieltherapie* [Non-Directive Game Therapy]), whose definition of a game is closest to my own:

> For Zullinger, the child is healed through the game itself; the therapist intervenes whenever there is a possibility of actively pushing ahead and developing the game further. The therapist can add his or her own impetus (in Zullinger's sense), produce material and arrange and structure a situation in a way he or she considers right. Thus the child is offered opportunities to use games to reduce emotional tensions and solve social conflicts. With the help of the therapist as game partner and through independent activities, these activities become increasingly constructive. In other words, Zullinger preferred pure game therapy—don't interpret for the child, but offer a great deal of variety of games and game practices.

The Role of the Group Leader

In the following quote, Jürgen Fritz (J. Fritz, *Methoden des sozialen Lernens* [Methods of Social Learning]) quotes Benita Daublensky's tips (B. Daublensky, *Spielen in der Schule* [Playing in School]) on the best ways for a group leader to achieve optimal results in games:

- Realize that you are not doing the children a favor.
- Help individuals without making them dependent on you.
- Protect children from difficulty without being overprotective. Let them create their own experiences as much as possible.
- Allow children to arrange themselves in pairs or groups as they wish, but help those who don't get chosen.
- Keep competition between children to a minimum.
- Create an open atmosphere and demonstrate to the children how they can help each other.

How to Use This Book

First Way: Going Step-By-Step

The games start with *I Games*. You can play some or all of the *I Games*, followed by *You Games*, and then *We Games*. Warm-up games for the group (listed in the index under "warming-up") can always be played at the beginning or in between the games. As children get better at the games in the first three sections, they can be introduced to the games in the last section, *Adding More Imagination*.

Second Way: Focusing on a Specific Problem

After a few warm-up games, start with any section that speaks to your concerns at the moment.

Example: You begin with Aggression Games as a way to approach the subject of aggression. Afterward, you look at it from a preventive perspective by playing Cooperation Games, Relationship Games, or Integration Games.

Third Way: Using the Follow-up Games

At the end of each game you will find suggestions for follow-up games. They either lead you to the games on the neighboring pages of the book or to games that have similar goals, playing methods, or player configurations.

Examples: You go from a partner game to another partner game. You go from drawing a picture with your partner in The Incredible Two-Handed Pen (Game #40) to helping your "blind" partner perform daily activities in Blindness in Everyday Life (Game #62). After a conversation game, you compare that game to a pantomime game. After a partner observation game, you play other perception games.

You can play the follow-up games in the given order. Alternatively, you can stick with any follow-up game you like and pursue the follow-up suggestions given there, going further off from the starting point while your game program gains variety.

A Brief Word on Brevity

If you're used to reading game instructions, you may be surprised that the ones in this book are so short. There is a reason for it.

When a group leader sticks too closely to a game's rules, following detailed playing instructions, his dependence on the rules can communicate itself to the group—to the detriment of all. In this book, I try to suggest games instead of prescribing them. Being too specific tends to limit the players and does not stimulate their creativity.

What if you, the game leader, don't completely understand the variations of a game? In that case, you will probably create your own variations—and that is as it should be. In my teacher-training seminars, I often give instructions that are intentionally brief. Inexperienced game players are often temporarily at a loss, but, necessity being the mother of invention, they soon begin to try out their own interpretations. When they ask "Now do we have to...?" or "Can we...?" I simply shrug—and watch their questions disappear as new games get created.

Not all eventualities and possibilities can be covered in a book such as this. Different groups will reach different ideas in different ways, all of them unpredictable. In my seminars, I usually play the basic version before I encourage students to invent alternate ones.

The approach and games in *101 More Life Skills Games for Children* can be combined well with the principles of "open learning," about which much has been written elsewhere.

Information about Simulation and Role-Play Games
In the last part of the book (Games 91–101), two specific categories of games are introduced that are more elaborate than the others. Additional information about the structure and goals of these games can be found on pages 144 and 149.

Key to the Icons Used in the Games

To help you find games suitable for a particular situation, the games are coded with symbols or icons. These icons tell you, at a glance, the following things about the game:

- The size of the group needed
- The level of difficulty
- If large space is needed
- If music is required
- If props are required
- If physical contact is or might be involved

These icons are explained in more detail below. Two icons included in other SmartFun books (age level and time) have been omitted here because the age group in this book is already clearly defined as children and teens ages 9–15 (exercises for children ages 6–12 can be found in *101 Life Skills Games for Children*) and because the duration of each game will vary depending on a number of factors including the size of the group and whether or not the particular game appeals to the players.

The size of the group needed. Most of the games are best played by a large group of players. If a game requires an even number of players or groups of 4 or 8, the game will be marked with the appropriate icon:

 = Even number 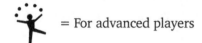 = Groups of 4

 = Groups of 8  = Game is suitable for a group of any size

The level of difficulty. The more complex games in this book that might be suited to older players are marked with the following icon:

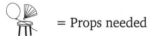 = For advanced players

If large space is needed. Almost every game in this book can be played in a classroom. The few games that require a larger space, such as a gym, are marked with the following icon:

= Large space needed

If music is required. Only a few games in this book require recorded music. If the music is optional, it is noted as such; if it is required, the icon below is used:

♪ = Music required

If props are required. Many of the games require no special props. In some cases, though, items such as chairs, instruments, paper and pens, or other materials are integral to running and playing a game. Games requiring props are flagged with the icon below, and the necessary materials are listed under the Props heading. Note that optional props will also be flagged (except when optional background music is the only item listed).

= Props needed

If physical contact is or might be involved. Although a certain amount of body contact might be acceptable in certain environments, the following icon has been inserted at the top of any exercises that might involve anywhere from a small amount of contact to minor collisions. You can figure out in advance if the game is suitable for your participants and/or environment.

 = Physical contact likely

I Games

What I'm Feeling
Games 1–10

What I'm Thinking
Games 11–12

How I Am
Games 13–21

A Picture of My Mood

Props: Cards with various pictures pasted on them

Goals
- Expressing moods and feelings
- Getting to know each other
- Overcoming shyness

How to Play: In the center of the circle are a lot of picture cards—two for every player. Each player chooses a picture that expresses her current mood. The players take turns explaining their choices.

Example: "I chose the picture of the deck chair because I'm tired and I wish I were sitting in a nice, comfortable chair."

Variation: Draw a mood picture.

Notes
- Not all players will automatically be aware of their current mood. You can help by pointing out that it doesn't have to be today's mood—they can talk about some other mood they've been in recently.
- If you as the game leader have no picture cards prepared, a day earlier you should ask each player to cut out two postcard-sized pictures from magazines—one for a positive mood, one for a negative one. The pictures can then be glued onto cards and even covered with clear contact paper to protect them.
- Once the players have played the game and they understand what the pictures are for, they'll enjoy helping you collect more of them.

Reflections
- What benefits are there to making ourselves aware of our moods?
- In what kinds of situations do you experience similar moods?
- Are you more affected by feelings (short-term) or moods (long-term)?

- How much is your mood influenced by the group?
- What could help you change your current mood?

Follow-up Games
2: Flashlight ◆ 13–21: How I Am ◆ 33: Favorite Place ◆ 34: Picture Present

Follow-up Games from *101 Life Skills Games for Children*
1–5: What I Like ◆ 41: Balloon Dance ◆ 52: Wake Up! ◆ 53: The Grouping Game ◆ 54: Hot Seat

Flashlight

Goals

- Expressing moods and feelings
- Introducing oneself and getting to know each other
- Overcoming shyness
- Verbalizing feelings

How to Play: The players agree on a theme or topic and try to describe their feelings about it.

Examples

If the theme is the weather:
- "There's a thunderstorm in me today."
- "I feel foggy."

If the theme is water:
- "I feel like Niagara Falls."
- "I'm a deep, still lake."

Note: In groups where students have speech problems or other difficulties expressing themselves, nonverbal "How Am I Feeling" games, such as Mood Meter (Game #3) are helpful preparation exercises.

Variation: The players agree on a material that is available that they can use to illustrate their moods. Then, for example, every player chooses a stone or a colorful cloth that corresponds to his mood.

Reflections

- Do you like expressing your moods to others?
- Have you found players who are in the same mood as you?

Follow-up Games

1: A Picture of My Mood and all of its suggested follow-up games ◆ 3: Mood Meter

3

Mood Meter

Props: Chairs

Goals
- Expressing moods and feelings
- Getting acquainted
- Overcoming shyness
- Verbalizing feelings
- Being helpful

How to Play: At a given signal, all the players stand up, stay sitting in their chairs, stand on their chairs, or sit on the floor—depending on how "high" their mood is. Players whose mood is at either extreme—whether they are in "high spirits" or feel very "down"—may be asked why.

Variation: After the players have guessed why a particular player's mood is extreme, she can tell the others if they are right.

Note: In this game, it is important to let the players volunteer to explain their moods. At first, it might be best to talk only to those players who are in a good mood. As game leader, you can always talk privately to the ones who are in bad moods.

Reflections
- What is the general mood of the group? Is your mood different from the mood of most of the group?
- Do you ever wish you could change your mood? Can the group help you? What could prevent you from talking to the group about your mood?
- Have you ever "hit rock bottom"? What makes you feel like you are "on cloud nine"?

Follow-up Games
All follow-up games suggested for 1: A Picture of My Mood ◆ 2: Flashlight ◆ 4: Body Language Spells Your Mood

4

Body Language Spells Your Mood

Goals

- Expressing moods and feelings
- Initiating communication
- Increasing physical awareness
- Increasing social awareness

How to Play: Each player takes a turn at using body language to show the group how they are feeling. Players can use a posture, a gesture, or a facial expression to convey these feelings.

Variation: Express your mood in a sentence.

Note: Some people find it hard to reveal their feelings through body language. And yet, the body is one of the most honest means of expression— body language doesn't lie. Often, what people say is the opposite of what their bodies tell us. In cases like that, usually it's the body that's telling the truth!

Reflections: How do you prefer to express your feelings: by showing your mood with words or through body language? Why not try both simultaneously sometime? In everyday life, they are usually combined. How does it feel when someone's words and body language disagree with each other?

Role Play: Whodunit?
A chosen "police detective" leaves the room.

Five players sit in a row at the front of the room. They decide among themselves which one of them is the "perp" who committed a crime.

Now the detective comes back in the room and starts asking questions of the five players. Naturally they all say they didn't do it. But the perpetrator, through facial expressions and body language, tries to show how a criminal's body language would give him away. The police detective tries to recognize which player is the perp.

Follow-up Games

3: Mood Meter ◆ 5: Moodles ◆ 21: Help Wanted ◆ 23: What's My Name ◆ 30: Heads Are Truthful, Tails Lie ◆ 36: Spy ◆ 80: Face-off ◆ 94: Shadow Play

Follow-up Games from *101 Life Skills Games for Children*

1–5: What I Like ◆ 27–32: Understanding You ◆ 78: Peace Language ◆ 83: Wolf in Sheep's Clothing ◆ 84–92: Statue and Sculpting Games ◆ 95: Fairytale Surprises ◆ 97–101: Pantomime Play

Moodles

Props: Paper and pens

Goals

- Expressing moods and feelings
- Reducing aggression
- Dealing with feelings
- Recognizing feelings
- Finding symbols for feelings

How to Play: Every player has a slip of paper and different pens to choose from and starts mood doodling—or moodling. What he or she moodles may not be a recognizable picture, but it's usually obvious whether the player was in a good or bad mood, tense or relaxed, happy, sad, or playful. The players show each other their moodles. They can also have the other players guess their moods. Players can be grouped by similar moods and moodles to create "mood posters."

Variations

- The game leader gives the players concrete instructions, such as "Draw an anger moodle."
- Players pair off and watch each other moodling. They recognize their partners' moods from the movements, facial expressions, and gestures they make while moodling.
- All moodle pictures are taped or pinned on a wall or board. Each player looks for a picture that best expresses his or her current mood.
- Players write sentences that express moods on slips of paper. Then they assign each sentence to a moodle.

Notes

- Moodling can serve to reduce aggressions. You can encourage aggressive children to moodle away their anger.
- Similarly, when there is a conflict in the class, the children can be asked to moodle away the incident.

Reflections

- Has moodling strengthened or weakened your feeling?
- What does a rage moodle look like? What do the lines and colors look like when you are happy?
- Do all your happy moodles look the same?
- Think of your handwriting in your exercise books: how do you write when you are angry and when you are in a good mood?

Role Plays

- Write an outraged letter to someone. Try to make your handwriting match your mood. Read aloud what you are writing.
- Also try a love letter.

Follow-up Games

4: Body Language Spells Your Mood ◆ 6: Mood Buildings ◆ 17: The "I" Museum ◆ 40: The Incredible Two-Handed Pen ◆ 80: Face-off ◆ 89: Statues as Mood Meters

Follow-up Games from *101 Life Skills Games for Children*

1: I Like This Picture ◆ 22: Gathering Names ◆ 78: Peace Language ◆ 97–101: Pantomime Play

Mood Buildings

Props: A set of blocks for each player

Goals
- Expressing moods and feelings
- Recognizing how the environment affects us
- Improving visual and tactile perception

How to Play: Each player is given a set of building blocks and makes a building that reflects his mood.

Variations
- Examples of other materials that could be used:
  Stones
  A selection of colored and patterned bandanas
  Glass beads
  Leaves
  Contents of a dollhouse
  Contents of a backpack
  Play-Doh
  Roots and twigs
  Flowers
  Dishes
  Several chairs

- Try to create a mood in this room that is cheerful or depressing.

Reflections
- Which material appeals to you most? Can you express certain moods particularly well with certain materials? Try and express two opposite moods with the same material. Can the material influence your mood?
- Does looking at the mood buildings of the other players influence your own mood?

- What do houses say about the people living in them? How do people's living environments influence their moods?

Follow-up Games

5: Moodles ◆ 7: Mood Mail ◆ 17: The "I" Museum ◆ 33: Favorite Place ◆ 67: Group-net ◆ 72: Stone Field

Follow-up Games from *101 Life Skills Games for Children*

1–5: What I Like ◆ 8–19: What I Observe ◆ 87: Statue Pairs

Mood Mail

Props: Pens and paper for all

Goals
- Expressing moods and feelings
- Getting to know the group's mood
- Sharing individual reflections nonverbally

How to Play: Players sit around in a circle. On a small slip of paper, each player writes down his mood in one sentence—without giving his name. The slips are passed around the circle until all players have their own slips again. Now they know the moods of the others in the group without knowing which is which, and they also have an impression of the general mood of the group. On another slip of paper, each player can write down her impression of the group's overall mood, which can be passed around the circle again.

Note: This method also provides the group leader with feedback. It is not very time-consuming. The game leader can keep the slips and go through them again at her leisure. Individual players can compare their own moods with the group's mood and try to adjust them.

Reflection: Since this game is usually played at the end of a series of games and serves as a kind of reflection in itself, no separate reflection is necessary.

Role Play: The mail carrier brings the mayor anonymous letters from the citizens' "Complaints Box."

Follow-up Games
6: Mood Buildings ◆ 8: Mood Music ◆ 11: Brainstorm ◆ 20: Pieces of Personality ◆ 32: See How You Are ◆ 67–73: Relationship Games

Follow-up Games *from 101 Life Skills Games for Children*
62: Emergency Kit

Mood Music

Props: Orff Instruments, such as tambourines, bongos, xylophones, drums, triangles, woodblocks, and metallophones (optional)

Goals
- Expressing moods and feelings
- Reducing aggression
- Improving acoustic perception
- Reducing inhibitions
- Learning to cooperate
- Being sensitive to tone of voice

How to Play: With the help of Orff Instruments, noises made with the body, such as snapping or clapping, or verbal sounds, the players take turns "telling" the group what their mood is.

Variations
- One player "says" (plays) something provocative; the other players respond by making noises to show how this statement affects them.
- The players express in one sentence what their mood is. They speak with altered voices: loud, quiet, shrill, dull, high, low, fast, slow, etc.
- The group leader assigns creative tasks (noise improvisations) to smaller groups of players. In a few minutes, they have invented an improvisation and present it to the other players: funeral march, wedding march, dance of joy, drum of death, drum of war, war cries, shouts of joy, love serenade, protest march, etc.
- If the group has access to a CD/cassette player and music, each group takes turns finding music samples for a particular mood, and the other groups guess what the mood is.

Reflections
- How do noises, sounds, tones, and music influence our mood?
- Name songs, bands, and types of music that express aggression, love, sadness, harmony, or chaos. How easily are you influenced by the different types of music?

- Name some everyday situations in which your mood is influenced by sound.

Follow-up Games

7: Mood Mail ◆ 9: Moodscapes ◆ 79: War Dance

Follow-up Games from _101 Life Skills Games for Children_

14: Seeing with Your Ears ◆ 38: Patty-Cake ◆ 47: Boom Box ◆ 61: Cry for Help ◆ 67: Crocodile Tears ◆ 75: Polite Wild Animals ◆ 81: Ghosts and Travelers ◆ 82: Vampire

Moodscapes

Props: Paper and pencils; dry erase board or chalkboard

Goals

- Expressing moods and feelings
- Getting to know each other and introducing oneself
- Becoming aware of feelings

How to Play: The game leader hands out a blank sheet of paper to each player. Then she tells the story below while sketching the scene on a dry-erase board or chalkboard, with the players copying the picture as well as they can on their own papers:

"In the middle of the sheet, from left to right, runs our day's path. When people feel neither good nor bad, they walk along this path during their day's journey. The path is completely straight. It's almost a little boring to walk along it. To the very left it's morning, and when you arrive at the very right it's evening.

"Above the path, there is a meadow with fresh grass. Whoever finds the path too boring and monotonous can run through the meadow, and her mood will immediately get better. The strip above the meadow is a gentle slope with flowers. If you walk along there, you can pick flowers and watch butterflies, bees, and beetles. Above this strip it gets hilly. There are different trees, brooks, all kinds of animals, and nice hiking trails. You feel relaxed and free there.

"If you climb higher, you go beyond the tree line. The mountains become steep. The scenery is now full of variety; waterfalls are splashing, mountain lodges invite you in; you climb peaks, enjoy the view and the peacefulness. You look down into the valley and feel happy to be up here—especially when you reach a peak and enjoy the proud feeling of accomplishing something not everybody can do.

"At the very top of our picture, there is the sky with clouds and birds. When we are up there, it's like a beautiful dream. Detached from the earth, we sit on top of a cloud and float along. Our freedom is boundless, all duties and worries far away—we are very happy.

"Now let's look at the picture below the day's path. It's sandy and rocky.

Almost nothing grows there. Walking on this path is very boring. Below this, there are big rocks lying around. You stumble a lot. Then comes a strip of marsh and undergrowth. You often have to make detours and hurt yourself. Sometimes you sink into the mud or step in a puddle. You don't feel at ease there at all. Further down is a jungle. Thorns and thick undergrowth make it almost impossible to make progress. Dangerous snakes scare you. It's damp, dark, and inhospitable. Whoever has to walk here can easily get lost and feel hopeless."

If she prefers, the game leader can just tell the story and hand out a photocopied version of the landscape. Whether the players have drawn the picture or just received it from the game leader, they now insert stick figures to indicate the level of their mood at different times of the day (today or the day before, see illustration). Finally, they draw a line from figure to figure. That way, the mood of the day becomes visible.

Reflections

- What does your line show? Is your mood mostly positive or negative? What do your highs and lows say about you? Can you describe your feelings at certain times of the day in more detail?
- What makes you happy and unhappy? Who can help you become happier? What can you do yourself?

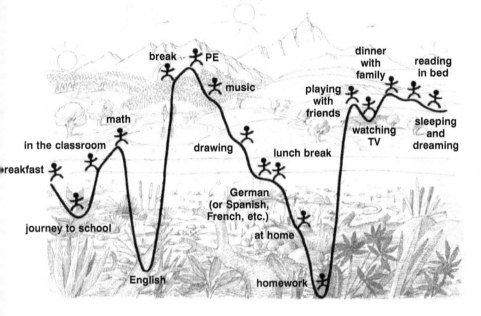

- Does each of your day curves look the same? Draw the curve of a day in which everything's okay.

Follow-up Games

8: Mood Music ◆ 10: Mood Dice ◆ 12: Finish My Thought ◆ 13–21: How I Am ◆ 22–34: Getting to Know You ◆ 35–39: Perceiving You ◆ 48: Lost in the Dark Woods ◆ 49: Stumbling over Roots ◆ 50: Through the Thicket ◆ 81: Gauntlet ◆ 88: Family Statues ◆ 96: Interview ◆ 100: Epic Game

Follow-up Games from *101 Life Skills Games for Children*

44: Good Morning! ◆ 52: Wake Up! ◆ 57–70: Helping Games

Mood Dice

Props: Mood dice, either purchased or made using the template at the end of this game

Goals
- Expressing moods and feelings
- Perceiving other people's feelings

How to Play: Each player throws the die until his own mood appears. Here are the six die images:

 The cheerful one is in a very good mood.

 The astonished one has just gotten a big surprise.

 The optimist knows that good things will happen.

 The pessimist thinks bad things will happen.

 The indecisive one doesn't quite know how he feels.

 The angry one is furious.

Variations
- Each player throws the die until he sees the mood he thinks one of the other players is in. He identifies the player, who then takes a turn.
- The game leader names an everyday situation. Each player throws the die until it shows the mood he thinks he would have in that situation.
- One player is chosen as the Guesser. All the other players make faces, and the Guesser has to guess which side of the die they are portraying. After she guesses five correctly, it's someone else's turn.

- One player throws the die three times. Now he or she tells a story that goes with the three faces.

Note: Make your own mood dice (see below), or look for similar ones at game stores or on the Internet. Try www.gamestation.net, then search for "mood dice."

Follow-up Games
9: Moodscapes ◆ 20 Pieces of Personality ◆ 32: See How You Are ◆ 35–45: Perceiving You ◆ 85–90: Statue and Sculpting Games

Follow-up Games from *101 Life Skills Games for Children*
30: You Draw Me ◆ 84–92: Statue and Sculpting Games ◆ 97–101: Pantomime Play

Brainstorm

Props: Paper and pens; background music (optional)

Goals
- Expressing thoughts without inhibition or fear of criticism
- Accepting other people's ideas without criticizing them
- Learning to think together

How to Play: Each player writes a "headline" on a sheet of paper. This can be a statement, a question, or a problem. The sheets are passed around in a circle. To the sheets they receive, the players add a "comment," which can be an opinion, a statement, a suggestion, or a question. In this way, a lot of different thoughts and ideas are generated quickly. The players should write down their comments without thinking about them too much, and they should not censor themselves or others. All ideas, no matter how impossible they seem and as long as they are not criticisms, are welcome for now—it's all part of the brainstorm.

Variations
- The sheets are put on chairs or tables that have been arranged in a circle. The players add their comments on the sheets in random order.
- The sheets are poster-sized and put up on the wall. The players write down their thoughts in big letters with thick markers. This is a good idea if the finished posters are to be discussed later on.
- In the middle of the room there is a big table or several smaller tables pushed together, covered with brown kraft paper. The players should be able to gather around the table easily. All players have pens and write down their comments, questions, opinions, or exclamations anywhere on the paper. At first, the comments will only refer to one of the headlines, but as more comments get added some of them will also refer to the other players' comments, and so on.

Reflection: Which comments have triggered thoughts in you?

Note: Soft music playing in the background can ensure a good atmosphere for this game.

Follow-up Games
7: Mood Mail ◆ 12: Finish My Thought ◆ 44: Two Writers, One Story ◆ 52–59: Cooperation Games ◆ 91–92: Simulation Games

Follow-up Games from *101 Life Skills Games for Children*
33–40: Working with You

Finish My Thought

Props: Paper and pens

Goal

- Expressing opinions

How to Play: Each player gets a piece of paper and tears it into sixteen slips of paper. Now the group leader says, "Number One. Ready?" and reads aloud the beginning of the first sentence. Then he pauses for a minute while each player numbers his own slip of paper and finishes the sentence in his own way. In this way, 16 sentence beginnings are read out loud, with a pause after each one to give the players time to number the slips and finish the sentences. The slips are then collected and sorted. Now the leader reads each sentence beginning and all of its different endings.

This game can be played for any number of topics. It's a good way to open up a discussion when there's a new topic to discuss.

Examples of Answers

From the topic of "school":
"At school, we should do more..."
"What I like about school is that..."
"What I like about our teacher is that..."

From the topic of "free time":
"I'd like to have more friends so that..."
"I like to play with..."
"In my free time my parents don't let me..."

From the sociopolitical area:
"Our environment would be better if..."
"When I'm grown up, I will..."

More Examples of Sentence Beginnings

1. At school, we should do more of...

2. What I like about school is . . .
3. What I like about our teacher is . . .
4. I don't want . . .
5. If I could wish for something impossible, it would be . . .
6. I like my best friend in class because . . .
7. In school, I'm afraid of . . .
8. I'm bored in school when . . .
9. School is fun when . . .
10. During snack I . . .
11. In the afternoon, when school is over, I . . .
12. We have fights in our class when . . .
13. I especially like being at school when . . .
14. During the next school vacation I want to . . .
15. My parents think that when I'm at school I . . .
16. If we didn't have school, . . .
17. When I enter the school building, I think of . . .
18. I'd like our teacher to . . .
19. I don't want our teacher to . . .
20. What I like about our class is that . . .
21. What I don't like about our class is that . . .
22. On our school trip . . .
23. For our school trip, I wish . . .
24. When I need help at school . . .
25. When someone else needs help . . .
26. School is hard work when . . .
27. The others don't like me when . . .
28. After school, I like to hang out with my friend because . . .
29. The worst day of school for me was when . . .
30. The best day of school for me was when . . .
31. I help other students with . . .
32. On the way to school . . .

Follow-up Games

11: Brainstorm ◆ 13–21: How I Am ◆ 22–34: Getting to Know You ◆
35–39: Perceiving You ◆ 46: Punctuation Mark ◆ 67–73: Relationship
Games ◆ 88: Family Statues ◆ 96: Interview ◆ 101: Personified Influences

Follow-up Games from *101 Life Skills Games for Children*

1–19: I Games ◆ 54: Hot Seat ◆ 56: Information Please ◆ 58: The
Comforter Game ◆ 59: The Helper Game ◆ 90: Class Picture

Missing Person

Props: Pens and slips of paper, and a box to draw them out of

Goals
- Strengthening self-image
- Admitting faults
- Emphasizing strengths

How to Play: Each player describes herself in three to five sentences on a slip of paper. All the slips are put into a box. One by one, players draw a slip from the box and try to guess who wrote it.

Note: In groups of people who don't know each other well yet, have the players include physical characteristics in their descriptions. When the players already know each other well, they can describe personality traits instead.

Reflections
- Was it difficult for you to describe yourself?
- Did any of the players admit their faults?

Follow-up Games
14: Who Said That? ◆ 22–34: Getting to Know You ◆ 35–39: Perceiving You ◆ 46–51: Warming-up Games for the Group ◆ 52–59: Cooperation Games ◆ 83: Agent Game ◆ 85–90: Statue and Sculpting Games

Follow-up Games from *101 Life Skills Games for Children*
27–32: Understanding You ◆ 41–45: Warming-up Games for the Group ◆ 53: The Grouping Game ◆ 84–92: Statue and Sculpting Games ◆ 93: Bad News and Good News Pairs

Who Said That?

Goals

- Strengthening self-image
- Training visual memory
- Getting acquainted

How to Play: This game is designed to be played by children who do not yet know each other. The players walk slowly around the room with their eyes closed. When the group leader shouts "Stop!" they stop, keeping their eyes closed. The leader taps one of the players on the shoulder, who then describes herself in a few sentences. At the command "Keep walking!" the players start to move again until they hear "Eyes open!" Now, who can find the person who just described herself?

Note: In groups whose members already know each other, the players may try to disguise their voices.

Follow-up Games

13: Missing Person and all of its suggested follow-up games ◆ 15: Celebrity Profile

Celebrity Profile

Props: Old magazines; scissors; glue; pens

Goals

- Strengthening self-image
- Recognizing the difference between ideal and reality
- Discovering common interests

How to Play: The group leader places a pile of old magazines on a table. With scissors, glue, and pens, all the players create a newspaper page about themselves. With a pen, they can start by altering an existing picture to look like them. Then they add suitable headlines. They can find a car, a house, a picture of an activity and their favorite food, and put it all together into a profile of how they would like to be.

Follow-up Games

All follow-up games suggested for 13: Missing Person ◆ 14: Who Said That? ◆ 17: The "I" Museum

Dream
People

Props: Pens and paper

Goals
- Strengthening self-image
- Recognizing the difference between ideal and reality
- Discovering common interests

How to Play: Each player designs two pictures of himself, one realistic and one idealized.

Variations
- Players create pictures of each other in pairs.
- The leader can collect all of the idealized pictures, and the players can take turns guessing who each picture represents.

Reflections
- It's not always easy to separate dream and reality. What was easier for you: to represent reality or your ideal?
- Do the real people resemble each other the most, or the dream people?

Follow-up Games
All follow-up games suggested for 13: Missing Person ◆ 14: Who Said That? ◆ 17: The "I" Museum

The "I" Museum

Props: Various favorite objects brought in by the players

Goals

- Strengthening the sense of identity
- Improving self-portrayal
- Presenting oneself to the group

How to Play: Each player has a table to use, her own corner of the room, and a small carpet or a space marked off in some other way where she can take up to 30 minutes to make an exhibit all about herself.

Some suggestions for exhibits:

Self-portrait, ID, photo, contents of pants pocket or bag, an essay or notes, a description of oneself in a few sentences, favorite object, nice stone ("this stone is precious to me because..."), a magazine clipping that mentions the person or says something about her indirectly, a lock of the player's hair, a watch, a piece of jewelry, a hair band, a shoe, a favorite flower, a drawing of a favorite TV show, the player's favorite food or favorite color, her lucky number....

Now it's time to visit the museum, and there are various ways to do it. For example, half of the players stay with their own exhibits and the other half spreads out to visit the different exhibits and have their creators explain them.

Variations

- The visitors walk through the exhibition as a group.
- Each exhibitor presents the exhibits as if they were made by a stranger
- Everyone walks through the room looking at the different exhibits on their own, without a guide.

Reflections

- How much did you reveal about yourself in the exhibition?
- Were some of the exhibitors honest about how they presented themselves?

- Did you get the impression that some exhibitors tried to make themselves look good?
- Which exhibits did you find particularly interesting?

Role Play: A celebrity guides a group of reporters through her apartment. The reporters ask questions about personal objects they see.

Follow-up Games
All follow-up games suggested for 13: Missing Person ◆ 15 Celebrity Profile ◆ 18: Trick or Trait

Trick or Trait

Props: Pens and paper

Goals
- Communicating personality traits
- Sharening social awareness

How to Play: The game leader chooses three volunteers and asks each one to choose an adjective that describes himself. They all whisper their adjectives into the game leader's ear. The adjectives should be traits that these players often exhibit. The game leader writes these adjectives on separate slips of paper, and then puts all three slips at the center of the circle so they can be seen by all players. The other players engage the three volunteers in a conversation and interview them on different topics. The volunteers try to answer the various questions in a way that helps the other players guess which quality they are portraying. After each question, the group guesses. Because the game can end very quickly, the players can take turns volunteering adjectives.

Variations
- The game leader assigns the qualities to the three volunteers.
- The players tell the volunteers about news headlines, to which they respond in a way that illustrates the selected qualities.

Reflections
- Do the qualities match their volunteers?
- Did the volunteers portray their qualities well?

Role Play: In advance, create "person," quality," and "situation" slips. To start, each player draws a "person slip" and a "quality slip." Then everyone pairs off, and each pair draws a "situation slip" and does a role-play based on their cards.

Example
Player A: "Grandfather," "good-natured."

Player B: "Small child," "high-spirited."
Situation slip: "They are both at the airport. One of them gets lost. Finally they find each other again."

In a further game phase, both players draw another person, quality, or situation slip.

Follow-up Games
17: The "I" Museum ◆ 19: Guess My Adjective ◆ 28: Two-Way Interview ◆ 30: Heads Are Truthful, Tails Lie ◆ 34: Picture Present ◆ 35–39: Perceiving You ◆ 53: Are You Like Me? ◆ 91–92: Simulation Games

Follow-up Games from *101 Life Skills Games for Children*
27: I Met My Match ◆ 44: Good Morning! ◆ 62: Emergency Kit ◆ 94: Fairytale Personalities ◆ 97–101: Pantomime Play

Guess My Adjective

Props: Cards with adjectives written on them

Goals
- Reacting to other people's personality traits
- Strengthening self-awareness

How to Play: Face down, at the center of the circle, there are six cards with one of the following adjectives written on them: funny, relaxed, pessimistic, serious, optimistic, and anxious.

A volunteer closes her eyes. Another player picks up one of the word cards and stands behind the volunteer so the other players can see it. Now everyone takes turns hinting to the volunteer what the card says. When she guesses correctly, whoever gave the most recent hint is the one who guesses next.

Example: If the card says "funny," hints might be as follows:
- "Ha-ha-ha"

- "cartoons and comedians"
- "a turtle falling in love with an army helmet"

Reflections
- Does the card held up behind you describe you?
- What's good and what's bad about having each of these qualities?

Follow-up Games
18: Trick or Trait and all of its suggested follow-up games ◆ 20: Pieces of Personality

Pieces of Personality

Props: Pens and slips of paper for all

Goals
- Expressing affection
- Comparing self-image with the way one appears to others
- Dealing with acceptance and rejection
- Getting acquainted
- Breaking the ice

How to Play: This game is suitable for children who do not yet know each other, but it can also be played if they do. All players fill out 5 to 10 slips of paper, each with a different personality trait. Then they move around the room handing the slips to each other. The players don't have to accept every slip they are offered—they can reject a trait they don't have or wish that they didn't have. Now, one by the one, the players go to the middle of the circle, tell what traits they've accepted, and try to act out those traits.

Reflections
- Did somebody feel wrongly labeled by many people?
- Who would like to correct the wrong image in front of the whole group?
- Which slips were you pleased about? Which slips made you angry?
- Has this game contributed to a good group spirit?

Follow-up Games
19: Guess My Adjective ♦ 21: Help Wanted

Help Wanted

Props: Pens and paper

Goals
- Training self-assessment
- Initiating communication

How to Play: Each player writes down five personality traits he thinks he has. Then he writes a job description for a job he needs done that requires these traits or qualities.

The players pair off and conduct job interviews. In each pair, one player is the employer and the other is the job seeker. In the end, each employer reports to the group how many of the specified qualities his job seeker had and whether he is going to hire him.

Reflection: Which qualities were most important for getting the job?

Follow-up Games
20: Pieces of Personality ◆ 28: Two-Way Interview ◆ 35–39: Understanding You

Follow-up Games from *101 Life Skills Games for Children*
6–7: What I Can Do ◆ 18: Collecting Sound Qualities ◆ 54: Hot Seat

You Games

Getting to Know You

Perceiving You

Working with You

The Story of My Name

Goals
- Strengthening self-identity
- Learning names
- Narrating
- Finding a partner
- Introducing oneself
- Introducing someone else

How to Play: Each player says his name and then tells a story about it.

Example: My name is Max. When I was at camp at age five the counselor said to me, "So your name is Max! We already have a Max here. He doesn't behave very well. I hope we'll be able to call you Good Max!" Well, they called me Good Max for a few days. Then the other Max and I became best friends, and for the rest of the summer the camp had two Bad Maxes!"

Variation: Each player chooses a partner to tell his story to. Now each player introduces his partner by telling the partner's "Story of My Name" to the group.

Reflections
- Do you like your name?
- What other name could you imagine for yourself?
- What other name would you rather have?
- What would you not like to be called?

Follow-up Games
23: What's My Name ◆ 52–59: Cooperation Games

Follow-up Games from *101 Life Skills Games for Children*
20–26: Getting to Know You ◆ 33–40: Working with You ◆ 43: Greeting Game ◆ 54: Hot Seat

What's My Name?

Goals
- Getting to know each other
- Introducing oneself
- Training visual memory
- Reducing inhibitions through movement

How to Play: This game is designed to be played by children who do not yet know each other. The players are divided into groups of seven to ten, depending on the age of the players and how well they can memorize. Each group forms a circle, and one by one the players make a distinctive movement or gesture while saying their own names. The other players then repeat the movement and the name. After everyone in the circle has said his name and demonstrated a gesture to go with it, go around the circle again and give everyone another chance to link up people's names with their gestures. Now the first player stands up and says, "What's My Name?" Players who think they remember it raise their hands. If they say the right name, the second player takes her turn, and so on.

Note: After the first round, the players can be regrouped so they can get to know others in the group.

Examples of Gestures
- Jump
- Crouch
- Spin
- Reach for the sky
- Cross hands in front of chest

Variation: One player tells a story in which members of the group appear. When he gets to a name, he replaces it with the movement the person made earlier. When the story is finished, the listeners name the players that appeared in the story.

Note: In terms of holistic learning, the simultaneous use of movement and language is of particular importance for remembering. Even after some time the movement a player made in this game comes to mind when one looks at them.

Reflection: Did the movement help you to remember the person's name? Were some names easier to remember because of the movement than others?

Follow-up Games
22: The Story of My Name ◆ 24: Name Riddles ◆ 36: Spy ◆ 85–90: Statue and Sculpting Games

Follow-up Games from *101 Life Skills Games for Children*
20–26: Getting to Know You ◆ 27–32: Understanding You ◆ 43: Greeting Game ◆ 52–56: Integration Games ◆ 78: Peace Language ◆ 84–92: Statue and Sculpting Games ◆ 97–101: Pantomime Play

Name Riddles

Props: Pens and blank cards to write on

Goals
- Learning names
- Training visual perception
- Stimulating creativity

How to Play: Players sit in a circle. Each player writes his name about 2 inches high on a card and puts it on the floor in front of him where everybody can easily read it. Now all the players take a minute to appreciate the special ways the different names are written. When everyone has looked at the names for a while, the cards are put in the center, and the group starts making up riddles about them. The other players try to be the first to grab the name card that answers the riddle.

Examples
"There's a name that has the name 'Anne' in it." (Answer: "Joanne")
"One name ends with a repeated letter." (Answer: "Matt")
"One name appears in the Bible and *Star Wars*." (Answer: "Luke")
"One name has only three letters." (Answer: "Eve")

Follow-up Games
23: What's My Name ◆ 25: Zip-Zap Names

Zip-Zap Names

Props: Chairs

Goals
- Initiating first contact
- Learning names
- Warming up
- Being considerate

How to Play: One player stands at the center of the chair circle. When she says "Zip!" all the other players shout the name of their own neighbor to the left, and when she says "Zap!" they shout the name of the neighbor to the right. When she says "Zip-Zap!" everyone swaps seats. The player in the middle tries to find a seat, too. Since there is one player more than the number of seats, one player is left without one. He is now at the center of the circle and he is the one who must say "Zip!" or "Zip-Zap!" or "Zap!"

Note: This game is excellent for warming up and bringing movement into the group. The quick seat change is also a good chance to practice consideration for others.

Follow-up Games
24: Name Riddles ◆ 26: Hello, Goodbye ◆ 35–39: Perceiving You ◆ 40–45: Working with You ◆ 46–51: Warming-up Games for the Group ◆ 52–59: Cooperation Games

Follow-up Games from *101 Life Skills Games for Children*
2: The Run-to Game ◆ 20–26: Getting to Know You ◆ 27–32: Understanding You ◆ 33–40: Working with You ◆ 41–44: Warming-up Games for the Group ◆ 52–56: Integration Games

Hello, Goodbye

Props: Pens and paper, and a box to collect them in

Goals
- Initiating first contact
- Maintaining poise while being at the center of attention
- Initiating communication

How to Play: Players write on a piece of paper how they would like people to greet and say goodbye to them. They also write their names on the paper. After all the papers have been collected and shuffled, one is selected and the person who wrote it leaves the room. When she comes back, the group greets her the way she has requested and then says goodbye in her favorite way. Of course, that means she has to leave the room again—but only for a minute!

Variation: All slips are in a box. Each player draws a slip, looks for its owner, greets her in the preferred way, and puts the slip back into the box. Then everyone draws a new one.

Examples
"My name is Kevin, and I'd like to be greeted with a hug."
"My name is Jeff, and you should say *Hi, Handsome!* when I come in the room."
"Pay me a compliment when you say '*Hello, Suzie!*'"

Reflections
- Did it happen the way you wanted it to? Would you wish for the same thing if you played the game again? Were there differences in the way different people granted your wish?
- Why aren't you always greeted that way in real life?
- Are there times when you prefer a formal "hello" and "good-bye" to an affectionate greeting?

Follow-up Games

25: Zip-Zap Names ◆ 27: Meet Me Halfway ◆ 45: Accidental Partners ◆
74: Something Nice

Follow-up Games from *101 Life Skills Games for Children*

3: Wishing Cards ◆ 23: Autograph Book ◆ 26: The Place on My Right Is
Empty (with a Twist) ◆ 33–40: Working with You ◆ 43: Greeting Game ◆
44: Good Morning! ◆ 52–56: Integration Games ◆ 62: The Emergency Kit

Meet Me Halfway

Props: Pens and oversized paper

Goals
- Strengthening group spirit
- Getting acquainted
- Discovering what we have in common

How to Play: Players pair off. Each pair has a piece of paper, and in the middle of it they draw the school (or meeting room). Now one player adds her home to the margin of the paper and explains to her partner how she gets to school, drawing her route on the paper as she explains it. Then it's the partner's turn to draw his house and his way to school. In the end, when they both know how they would travel to visit each other, they can meet each other halfway—on paper!

Variation: All players position themselves in the room according to the actual geographical location of their homes—for example, those who live to the north stand north of the rest of the class Neighbors stand next to each other. Those who live closer to school stand near the middle of the room, where the teacher is sitting. Now players can visit each other and comment, for example, "If I want to visit Joanne, I pass by Megan and Luke."

Follow-up Games
26: Hello, Goodbye ◆ 28: Two-Way Interview ◆ 39: Two Peas in a Pod ◆ 40–45: Working with You ◆ 46–51: Warming-up Games for the Group ◆ 52: Come into the Circle

Follow-up Games from *101 Life Skills Games for Children*
27–32: Understanding You ◆ 33–40: Working with You ◆ 53: The Grouping Game

Two-Way Interview

Props: Pens and slips of paper

Goals
- Having a conversation
- Getting to know each other
- Practicing honesty
- Achieving closeness and distance in a conversation

How to Play: Each player writes on a slip of paper five questions she would like to ask another player. The players pair off and ask each other the questions.

Eventually everybody sits down in a circle of chairs. The rest of the group interviews each pair with questions about their partners, such as "What's your partner's name?" or "What size shoe does she wear?" The more questions the pair can answer about their partners, the better.

Variation: After the two-way interview, each player finds a new partner and starts a conversation, which goes a bit like this: "I saw you talking to the girl with the long blond hair. What did you talk about? Tell me about her!"

Reflections
- Does it make a difference for you if someone interviews you or if you have to talk about yourself in front of the whole group?
- How do you feel when somebody talks about you when you are there?
- Were you asked questions that you couldn't or didn't want to answer? Why couldn't or didn't you?
- Are there questions you were afraid to ask?
- Did you answer some questions incompletely or dishonestly? Why?

Follow-up Games
27: Meet Me Halfway ◆ 29: Disposable Secrets ◆ 38: 20 Questions ◆ 46: Punctuation Mark

Follow-up Games from *101 Life Skills Games for Children*
54: Hot Seat

Disposable Secrets

Goals

- Getting acquainted
- Trusting
- Handling secrets
- Understanding group spirit

How to Play: The group leader has the players walk around the room whispering, to everyone they encounter, something that could be a secret (for example: "I'm going to tell you a secret: I'm going to Hawaii this summer!" or "Did you know I'm moving in a month?")

After a few minutes the players give the secrets of their fellow players away (for example: "Did you know that Rick was going to Hawaii this summer?" or "I know a secret about Barbara. I'm not going to tell you. Okay, I'll tell you—she's moving in a month!")

Note: It has to be made clear before the game starts that this is a role play in which the rules allow the players to tell each other's secrets. But after the game, the group should talk about when it's good to keep a secret in real life, and when it's okay not to.

Reflections

- What is it like to tell a secret? Who can you trust?
- Has anyone ever betrayed your trust?
- Am I too trusting? Am I trustworthy?
- In the game, who felt awkward telling a secret?
- Did you worry about telling secrets?
- When you told a secret, did you tell the kind of thing that's usually a secret or was it just a harmless fact?
- What connection is there between group spirit and sharing secrets?

Role Plays

- I'll never tell you a secret again!

- A criminal confesses his crime to his best friend. What should the friend do?

Follow-up Games
28: Two-Way Interview ◆ 30: Heads are Truthful, Tails Lie ◆ 31: Rumor Factory

Follow-up Games from *101 Life Skills Games for Children*
56: Information Please ◆ 59: The Helper Game

Heads Are
Truthful, Tails Lie

Props: Pens and paper for all

Goals
- Getting to know each other
- Handling truth and lies
- Practicing communicative questions

How to Play: Each player writes down six questions that he's going to ask the other players in order to get to know them better. The questions are numbered 1 to 6 (see examples below). Now the players pair off. In each pair, one partner asks a question and flips a coin. If the coin shows tails, the other partner has to answer the question truthfully ("I don't want to answer that" is also a truthful answer). If the coin comes up heads, the question has to be answered with a lie.

Examples
1. How many brothers and sisters do you have?
2. Do you live near anyone in this room?
3. How much allowance do you get?
4. What made you very angry recently?
5. What makes you really sad?
6. What's your favorite joke?

Variations
- The game can also be played with the whole group sitting in a circle. They spin a bottle, and whomever the bottle points to will answer the question. Then the coin is flipped.
- One player doesn't know whether the coin has come up heads or tails. She has to guess whether the questions have been answered truthfully or not. In order for this player not to know, she can close her eyes while the result of the coin toss is indicated to the group with a "thumbs up" for heads or "thumbs down" for tails.

Reflections

- Did you find it difficult to lie?
- Do you wish you always knew when someone was lying?
- Are there questions that make you want to say, "I'm not telling," "I don't know," or "I can't answer that"?
- How can body language let you know when someone isn't telling the truth?

Role Plays

- The white lie
- Tell it to the judge!
- The guilty conscience

Follow-up Games

29: Disposable Secrets ◆ 31: Rumor Factory ◆ 101: Personified Influences

Follow-up Games from *101 Life Skills Games for Children*

54: Hot Seat

Rumor Factory

Goals
- Getting to know each other
- Dealing with rumors
- Passing on facts correctly
- Telling the truth

How to Play: Separate the players into groups of four. The groups play separately. For each group, Player 1 and Player 2 go to a corner of the room, where Player 2 interviews Player 1, asking her several questions. Then Player 1 leaves, and Player 2 reports the results of the interview to Player 3. Now Player 3 reports what she has heard to Player 4. Player 4 reports back to the other three players what he thinks Player 1 said in the original interview. Finally, when Player 1 tells them what she really said, the group can see how much information is missing and what got added or changed along the way.

Variation: The description of a picture is retold from person to person.

Reflections
- How do rumors start?
- How does information change in the telling?
- What are some popular rumor topics in everyday life?
- Was there ever a rumor about you?
- How can you keep from inventing or continuing a bad rumor?
- Can a prejudice cause a rumor?

Follow-up Games
30: Heads Are Truthful, Tails Lie ◆ 32: See How You Are ◆ 77: Circle of Threat ◆ 81: Gauntlet

Follow-up Games from *101 Life Skills Games for Children*
79: Rumors

See How You Are

Props: Pens and paper

Goals
- Getting to know each other
- Learning to describe someone else
- Improving verbal communication
- Training social and visual awareness

How to Play: Players pair off to interview each other about age, family, hobbies, personality traits, likes and dislikes, etc. They write the results in a few sentences on a sheet of paper. On the back of the sheet, they also briefly describe the person's physical features.

The sheets are then exchanged with other players. Reading the front of the sheet first, they try to guess who the person is. If they can't figure it out, they look at the other side.

Follow-up Games
31: Rumor Factory ◆ 33: Favorite Place ◆ 35–39: Perceiving You ◆ 54: We Are Alike

Follow-up Games from *101 Life Skills Games for Children*
30: You Draw Me ◆ 84–92: Statue and Sculpting Games

Favorite Place

Goals
- Getting to know each other better
- Strengthening visual memory
- Making someone happy

How to Play: In pairs, players describe their favorite place to each other. It can be in their home (a chair, a room, one corner of a room), outdoors (a bench in the backyard, a spot under a specific tree, a viewpoint, a grassy meadow) or in a public space (a spot in the classroom, downtown, or in the park). The partner should have enough information to be able to draw the described spot without help. The partners draw each other's favorite spot and present it to each other as a gift.

Variations
- Each player tells his partner how it feels to be at his favorite spot: what he can see from there, what noises he hears, how it smells there, if it's warm or cold, what thoughts come up.
- In groups of four, the players report about their partners' favorite places. The listeners have their eyes closed and try to feel and experience everything the way it is for the narrator.

Reflections
- Is there any one quality that's common to every favorite place?
- What would happen if everybody had the same favorite place?
- Has anyone ever disturbed a spot that you wanted to have for yourself?
- Are there places where you like to hang out with certain other people?

Follow-up Games
32: See How You Are ♦ 34: Picture Present ♦ 40–45: Working with You ♦ 56: Designing a Classroom

Follow-up Games from *101 Life Skills Games for Children*
1–5: What I Like ♦ 10: Changing the Room ♦ 45–51: Cooperation Games ♦ 57–70: Helping Games

Picture Present

Props: Pictures with a wide range of subject matter—nature, people, housewares, etc.

Goals

- Initiating contact
- Making someone happy
- Learning to accept a gift

How to Play: On a large table, picture cards are spread out—twice as many cards as there are players. The cards show landscapes, objects, people, dishes, plants, animals, or events. Players choose pictures to give as gifts to other players, indicating why they have chosen the picture. The person who has been given the present thanks the other player for the gift. He can explain why he is happy about it, or why he thinks it's not really the gift for him. The gifts can be passed on.

Example: "I'm giving you this private house at the ocean because I believe you like to be near water and you sometimes like to be by yourself."

Reflections

- Do you like giving presents?

- What kind of presents do you like most?
- How do you find out what other people like?
- Has someone ever given you a gift without seeming to care?

Role Play: The wrong gift. Someone gives you a horrible gift (for example, a fake eyeball) and you pretend it's just what you've always wanted.

Follow-up Games
33: Favorite Place ◆ 35–39: Perceiving You ◆ 67–73: Relationship Games ◆ 74: Something Nice

Follow-up Games from *101 Life Skills Games for Children*
3: Wishing Cards ◆ 57–70: Helping Games

Yes No
Yes No

Props: Pens and slips of paper

Goals
- Comparing self-image with how others see us
- Discovering similarities

How to Play: Each player has five slips of paper. On three of them, she writes a personal question that can be answered YES or NO. These slips are put into the center. On the forth slip everyone writes the word YES, and on the fifth the word NO.

Now the first player draws a slip and reads out the question. Then she puts her answer slip YES or NO face down in front of her. The other players guess if she has answered the question with YES or NO and then put the corresponding slip face down in front of them. Now the players turn over their slips one by one and explain why they thought the first player would have answered that way. In the end, the question reader also turns over her answer slip.

Examples
- Do you have any brothers or sisters?
- Do you play soccer?
- Do you have a dog?

Reflections
- Do the others not know me well?
- Why can't they guess my answers?
- Do I want to be predictable?
- How can I be less mysterious?
- How can I keep others from knowing too much about me?
- What are the disadvantages if others don't know us very well?

Follow-up Games

13–21: How I Am ◆ 28: Two-Way Interview ◆ 32: See How You Are ◆ 33: Favorite Place ◆ 34: Picture Present ◆ 36: Spy ◆ 46: Punctuation Mark ◆ 85–90: Statue and Sculpting Games ◆ 93–101: Social Role-Play Games

Follow-up Games from *101 Life Skills Games for Children*

62: Emergency Kit

Spy

Props: Pens and index cards for all players

Goals

- Learning about how others see us
- Training social awareness

How to Play: This game is meant to be played with other games. All players write their first name on an index card. The cards are shuffled, and then each player draws one and keeps it hidden from the other players. He now has to secretly observe his "target" while some other games are played. After the games, players report some of their observations to the whole group.

Reflection:

- What did you observe?
- How active was your target in the games?
- What did your target do and say?
- What particular things did you notice about your target's clothes, language, and movements?

Variation: Only a few students are spies, and they don't play the games. The players know who the spies are but don't know who their targets are.

Role Play: A player has observed something suspicious. He tells the group leader what he has seen. A suspect now gets accused of terrible things, but it turns out they didn't really happen.

Follow-up Games

35: Yes No Yes No ◆ 37: Animals' Toolbox ◆ 54: We Are Alike ◆ 85–90: Statue and Sculpting Games ◆ 93–101: Social Role-Play Games

Follow-up Games from *101 Life Skills Games for Children*

29: You Reflect Me ◆ 53: The Grouping Game ◆ 78: Peace Language

Animals' Toolbox

Props: Pens and slips of paper

Goals
- Comparing self-image with how others see us
- Training social awareness

How to Play: Each player gets one slip of paper. She thinks of an animal, and then writes the name of a plant and a tool the animal reminds her of and also the color the animal might be. After the slips are collected and shuffled, they are drawn from the pile one by one. Everybody guesses which animal was being thought of, and then the owner of the slip identifies herself and explains how everything goes together.

Example: Giraffe, tall tree, ladder, yellow. The owner might say, "A tall tree is something only a giraffe can nibble on, a ladder is a tool that helps us to reach higher like a giraffe, and yellow is the color of a giraffe."

Follow-up Games
1–10: What I'm Feeling ◆ 13–21: How I Am ◆ 36: Spy ◆ 38: 20 Questions

Follow-up Games from *101 Life Skills Games for Children*
1–5: What I Like ◆ 27–32: Understanding You

20 Questions

Props: Pens and slips of paper

Goals
- Learning how others see us
- Getting acquainted

How to Play: One player writes down the name of another player, concealing it from view. All the players take turns guessing the name of the person by asking questions about him. As soon as the answer to one of the questions is "No," it's another person's turn to ask.

Examples
- Is the person female?
- Is the person wearing something red?
- Is the person often late?

Reflections
- Did this game say anything about how well or how little the other players know you? Do you want them to know you better?
- Do you get the feeling that most players know you pretty well?
- What can you do to help others know more about you?

Follow-up Games
37: Animals' Toolbox ◆ 39: Two Peas in a Pod ◆ 96: Interview

Follow-up Games from *101 Life Skills Games for Children*
54: Hot Seat

Two Peas in a Pod

Goals
- Sharpening visual awareness
- Making friends
- Improving group spirit and solidarity

How to Play: All players walk around the room. They stop in front of everyone they encounter and say what physical features they have in common, then say "We're Two Peas in a Pod."

Examples
"You have brown eyes like I do. We're Two Peas in a Pod."
"We both have a digital watch. We're Two Peas in a Pod."
"We are the same height. We're Two Peas in a Pod."

Reflection
- Try to notice people's similarities in everyday life. What do certain groups of people have in common? Do you know people outside of the group you have a lot in common with?
- Do you know of groups that dress alike on purpose, or have the same hairstyle? Do you know people who talk like each other?
- Why do people cultivate a "group spirit" and want to dress the same or talk like each other? Can you think of any disadvantages to this?

Role Play: Initiation into a youth group. The candidate is tested on how similar her tastes are to the group norm. She must conform! For example, she has to like the same breakfast cereal and watch the same TV shows.

Follow-up Games
38: 20 Questions ◆ 52–59: Cooperation Games ◆ 67–73: Relationship Games ◆ 77: Circle of Threat ◆ 85–90: Statue and Sculpting Games

Follow-up Games from *101 Life Skills Games for Children*
1–5: What I Like ◆ 27: I Met My Match ◆ 39: Twins ◆ 50: Tug of War ◆ 77: Frontline ◆ 84–92: Statue and Sculpting Games

The Incredible Two-Handed Pen

Props: Pens and oversized paper

Goals
- Working together
- Putting yourself in another's shoes
- Communicating nonverbally

How to Play: The group leader divides the group into pairs. Each pair shares a pen and a large sheet of paper. Together, silently, they draw a picture—both holding the pen at the same time. They have five minutes.

Variations
- The game leader gives the players a theme—house, kite, ship.
- The two players agree on a theme before they start to draw.
- They don't agree on a theme, and wait and see what emerges.

Reflections
- Did you have a partner who was too bossy?
- What can you do to have a good collaboration?
- What qualities and behavior prevent good teamwork?

Follow-up Games
41: The Incredible Two-Headed Artist ◆ 43: Flying Colors ◆ 52–59: Cooperation Games ◆ 62: Blindness in Everyday Life ◆ 85: Frozen Pairs ◆ 93–101: Social Role-Play Games

Follow-up Games from *101 Life Skills Games for Children*
27–32: Understanding You ◆ 33–40: Working with You ◆ 45–51: Cooperation Games ◆ 57–70: Helping Games

41

The Incredible Two-Headed Artist

Props: Pens and oversized paper

Goals
- Practicing teamwork
- Putting yourself in another's shoes
- Communicating nonverbally

How to Play: The group leader divides the players into pairs. Each pair gets a pen and a large sheet of paper. Without talking, Player A starts to draw. She continues drawing for about 10 to 20 seconds until Player B takes the pen from her and starts to draw. After another 10 or 20 seconds, Player A takes over again, and so on. As soon as one player thinks the drawing is finished, the game is over for that pair.

Reflections
- Did you draw one picture together, or did two separate pictures emerge?
- Who was more guided by the other's ideas? Are both happy with the end result, or did one of you feel that you had to compromise your ideas?
- Are there any situations in everyday life where there is silent agreement, and two people can function together without discussing it?

Follow-up Games
40: The Incredible Two-Handed Pen
◆ 42: We're on the Same Page
◆ 43: Flying Colors

We're on the Same Page

Props: Pens and oversized paper

Goals
- Practicing teamwork
- Getting acquainted
- Putting oneself in another's shoes
- Making room for someone else
- Being able to set boundaries
- Achieving peaceful coexistence

How to Play: All players get a pen and pair off. In each pair, both players simultaneously start drawing on the same sheet of paper. Some players will doodle, some will just let their pen roam around on the paper, and others will start with an abstract or concrete image. Sometimes, the pens of the players will meet—accidentally or deliberately. Each pair will either coordinate their activities or try to avoid bumping into each other. When they're finished, both players name their drawings as if they were one piece of art—a drawing isn't finished until the two partners can agree on a name!

Note: It's good for players to play this game several times with different partners so they can have different partnership experiences.

Reflections
- Which partner did you harmonize with best?
- Is agreement the most important thing, or can differing ideas some-times create a more interesting drawing?

Follow-up Games
All follow-up games suggested for 40: The Incredible Two-Handed Pen ◆ 41: The Incredible Two-Headed Artist ◆ 43: Flying Colors ◆ 44: Two Writers, One Story

Flying Colors

Props: Pens for all—half the players get pens with one ink color, the other half get a different color

Goals
- Practicing teamwork
- Getting acquainted
- Putting oneself in another person's shoes
- Making room for someone else
- Being able to set boundaries
- Achieving peaceful coexistence

How to Play: This game is an excellent follow-up to We're on the Same Page (Game #42). Players pair off. The two players in each pair use pens of different colors and simultaneously start drawing on the same sheet of paper. Some players will doodle and draw their own pictures, and some may discover they can draw the same pictures with two different colors. When they're finished, each pair must agree on one name for their drawings.

Reflections
- What happens when the two colors overlap? Did you draw separate pictures or did you try to harmonize your colors in some way?
- When people look at your drawings, what can they say about your collaboration with your partner?

Follow-up Games
All follow-up games suggested for 40: The Incredible Two-Handed Pen ◆ 41: The Incredible Two-Headed Artist ◆ 44: Two Writers, One Story

Two Writers, One Story

Props: Pens and paper

Goals
- Practicing collaboration
- Fostering creativity
- Improving linguistic dexterity
- Working out divisions of labor
- Learning the dynamics of a partnership
- Accomplishing something together

How to Play: Players pair off and, together, each pair writes down a story on a piece of paper, taking turns adding words. They can alternate either after every word or after every two or three words. They are not allowed to influence each other, and players should not spend too much time thinking, instead writing down what comes to their minds first. The stories are read to the group when complete or after a predetermined time has elapsed.

Variation: Within a pair, each player is responsible for specific kinds of words. For example:

Player A provides all verbs, articles, adjectives.

Player B provides all nouns, conjunctions, prepositions, pronouns.

All other words can be discussed and used by both players. Player A begins (often with an article)

Example:
One (A) day (B), the (A) father (B) went (A) with (B) his (B) dear (A) wife (B) . . .

Note: For students whose understanding of the parts of speech is less advanced, the group leader may simply divide the words into more easily recognized groups such as nouns, verbs, modifiers, and "small words." This game is not about grammar; it is about recognizing that in working together as partners, different skills can be used to accomplish something together. It's also about letting your partner do her share of the work and not interfering with what she is doing.

Variations
- The game leader sets the theme for the story, for example a well known fairy-tale.
- The two players make up a story in which they are the two main characters.

Reflections
- Was your partner a help or a problem? If he didn't help, did you still have fun? In a game that nobody can win or lose, what makes it fun?
- Are there situations in which you work with adults who don't appreciate your contribution?

Follow-up Games
All follow-up games suggested for 40: The Incredible Two-Handed Pen ◆ 42: We're on the Same Page ◆ 45: Accidental Partners

Accidental Partners

Props: Pens, slips of paper, and a box to draw them from

Goals
- Learning to cooperate with a partner
- Recognizing and rethinking stereotypes
- Tolerance in teamwork
- Patience with partners
- Poise in winning and losing

How to Play: Before the players know what this game is about, the game leader asks them to think of partners in the group they can imagine working well with. Each player writes on a piece of paper, considering whom she has thought of, the sort of partner and the qualities and traits she thinks would make things go smoothly. The players keep these pieces of paper for later discussion. Now the players are evenly divided into Groups A and B. All the players in Group A are assigned a consecutive number. Similarly numbered slips are put into a box for shuffling, and then all the players in Group B draw a slip—that's their Accidental Partner. Several tasks are written on the board, and the partners have to choose one and do it together. The partners have an organizing session in which they discuss good teamwork and how to tackle the tasks: Who takes over which jobs? What are they going to tackle together and what tasks are they going to divide up?

Examples
- Build the tallest possible tower out of 30 building blocks.
- Solve the following six math problems, showing your work.
- Find words in a certain category, to be announced at the start of the game, such as "Write down all objects you can see here that start with the letter A!"

To Determine the Winner: For a missing or incorrect math problem, points are deducted. The players get one point for each block of the tower, three for every word in a word field, and five for each correct calculation. For building the tallest tower they get three additional points, for the second tallest tower they get two, and for the third tallest they get one additional point.

Reflections
- Were you disappointed not to get the partner you wanted?
- How did your partner react when you told him your ideas about good partners?
- How did your planning meeting go?
- Did your partner take his assigned tasks seriously? What was it like working with him?
- How did your partner react to the end result? What effect did this re-action have on you?

Variation: Now each player can play the game with a partner of her choice. New math problems and a new category—maybe words starting with a new letter?—are assigned.

Role Plays
- No, I don't want to sit next to you!
- Boss, it's impossible to work with this guy!

Follow-up Games
All follow-up games suggested for 40: The Incredible Two-Handed Pen ◆ 44: Two Writers, One Story

We Games

Warming-up Games for the Group

Cooperation Games

Integration Games

Relationship Games

Aggression Games

Punctuation Mark

Props: Set of posters each showing a different punctuation mark

Goals

- Warming up
- Starting a conversation
- Overcoming shyness

How to Play: The players walk around the room to soft music—either a recording or the group leader playing an instrument. Suddenly the game leader stops the music and holds up a poster showing a large punctuation mark. The players start talking to each other in a style related to the mark: excitedly if it's an exclamation point, curiously if it's a question mark, hesitantly if it's an ellipsis. The music starts again, and the players stop talking until the next punctuation mark is held up.

Examples

Exclamation Point $\boxed{!}$
The players shout to each other as they walk, for example: "Hey, Hillary!" "Come on, let's walk together!" "Don't walk so fast!" "That's ridiculous!"

Question Mark $\boxed{?}$
The players ask each other questions, such as "How are you?" "What's your name?" "Do you like this game?"

Period $\boxed{\cdot}$
The players make statements, declarations, or tell each other things like: "I like this game." "I'm bored." "I'd like to have a break now." "I like you."

Follow-up Games
47: Name Chain ◆ 85–90: Statue and Sculpting Games

Follow-up Games from *101 Life Skills Games for Children*
41–44: Warming-up Games for the Group ◆ 45–51: Cooperation Games ◆ 52: Wake Up! ◆ 84–92: Statue and Sculpting Games

Name Chain

Goals
- Warming up
- Initiating contact
- Getting to know names

How to Play: Two groups are formed. Group A, the guessing group, leaves the room. Group B forms a line. It is a line of names, for example David, Vanessa, José, Latisha, Ahmad, Mei, and Erica. Everyone has to remember which name comes after his in the chain. Now the players in Group B start to wander around the room randomly.

The guessing group comes back, and the game leader explains that they have to visit each member of Group B in the right order (i.e., the chain of names originally formed). The members of the guessing group only get the name of the first person, in our case "David," as a hint. This is a contest, so the members of Group A search as fast as they can. They run from one player in Group B to the next and whisper into their ears: "Are you David?" Everybody says no, except David. He says, "Yes, I'm David, now look for Vanessa!" The player who reaches Erica first, after asking her way through the whole line of names, is declared the winner by Erica.

Note: For many players, this game sounds complicated at first, but as soon as the game gets going, everybody knows what to do. This game is a lot of fun; the only reason it can't be played many times is that it's such an excellent way to learn names! But players who already know each other's names will also enjoy playing variations of this game.

Variation: Members of Group B take on animal names.

Follow-up Games
46: Punctuation Mark ◆ 48: Lost in the Dark Woods

Lost in the Dark Woods

Goals
- Warming up
- Being comfortable with body contact
- Learning to trust
- Reducing fear

How to Play: Two groups are formed. Members of Group A position themselves in the room spreading their arms. These players represent trees. There should be a distance of 2 to 3 yards between "trees."

Players of Group B try to feel their way through the dark woods with their eyes closed by holding onto branches at every step.

Note: Initially, not all players manage to keep their eyes closed tight. Sometimes they peek. Some players are afraid of the dark, so peeking a little is okay. If they are used to playing "blind games," it won't be a problem—they will know that "blind games" are more fun with eyes closed.

Role Plays
- A group of people gets lost in a place they cannot get out of. What should they do? Keep wandering about? Should a few try to get help while the others stay put?
- In the basement of a huge, unfamiliar house the light suddenly goes out.

Follow-up Games
47: Name Chain ◆ 49: Stumbling over Roots ◆ 59: Space Expedition ◆ 60: Seeing with Your Fingertips

Follow-up Games from *101 Life Skills Games for Children*
41–44: Warming-up Games for the Group ◆ 55: I'm Here! ◆ 81: Ghosts and Travelers ◆ 82: Vampire

any
size

Stumbling over Roots

Goals
- Warming up
- Initiating body contact
- Reducing fear
- Developing trust
- Being considerate

How to Play: Two groups are formed. The players of Group A lie on their stomachs, widely spreading their arms and legs so they are touching each other with their hands and feet. In this way, they form a net on the floor. The players of Group B now try to get through this "forest" with their eyes closed, without stepping on or stumbling over the roots.

Note: As in Lost in the Dark Woods (Game #48), some players have to peek to overcome the obstacles. Also, the players lying on the floor can practice keeping their eyes closed, trusting that nobody will hurt them.

Variation: Three groups are formed. The players of Group C lead the "blind" players of Group B while Group A lies on the floor.

Follow-up Games
48: Lost in the Dark Woods and all of its suggested follow-up games ◆ 50: Through the Thicket

Through the Thicket

Goals
- Warming up
- Developing trust
- Reducing fear

How to Play: Players divide into two groups. By stretching out their arms and legs out wide, the players in Group A position themselves in a way that forms a thicket. They can take each other's hands; some kneel, some crouch, and some stand upright. They form a tangle of branches, trunks, leaves, and spaces in between, which is then explored by the players of Group B, first by day (with eyes open), and then by night (with eyes closed).

Variations
- The explorers go in pairs and can't let go of each other while penetrating the thicket.
- The explorers can cut through entwined twigs (by disentangling the hands), but the gaps close up again right afterwards.

Follow-up Games
All follow-up games suggested for 48: Lost in the Dark Woods ◆ 49: Stumbling over Roots ◆ 51: The Goofy Game

The Goofy Game

Goals

- Warming up
- Reducing fear
- Developing trust
- Creating group spirit

How to Play: All players walk about "blindly"—with their eyes closed—throughout the game. The game leader inconspicuously taps a player to be the "Goofy." All players try to find the Goofy. They ask each player they encounter while walking around, "Goofy?" The other player asks the same question. The player who actually comes across the Goofy does not get a response. Now she knows who the Goofy is. She takes the hand of the Goofy

and is now a Goofy as well. If someone touches her and asks if she is the Goofy, she doesn't give an answer, either. The new Goofy joins them. That way a long Goofy line forms that moves through the room. In the end, all players have become Goofies.

Note: Not all players immediately understand the game instructions that the game leader gives. Sometimes a test run is necessary for this game.

Follow-up Games

All follow-up games suggested for 48: Lost in the Dark Woods ◆ 50: Through the Thicket

Come into the Circle

Goals

- Becoming integrated into the group
- Enhancing group spirit
- Strengthening visual perception

How to Play: The players form a circle with one player at the center. He calls to another player who he shares something in common with, such as a physical feature. The second player joins the first player in the circle. Then the second player summons a third player whom she feels she has something in common with. During the summoning, the common feature is always stated out loud. The game is played until all players are inside the circle.

Example

Mike says, "Briana, come into the circle because you have long hair like me!"

Then Briana says, "Riley, come into the circle because you're tall, like me!"

Then Riley says, "Luca, come into the circle because you and I are both wearing jeans!"

Follow-up Games

40–45: Working with You ◆ 46–51: Warming-up Games for the Group ◆ 53: Are You Like Me? ◆ 67–73: Relationship Games

Follow-up Games from *101 Life Skills Games for Children*

20–26: Getting to Know You ◆ 33–40: Working with You ◆ 41–44: Warming-up Games for the Group ◆ 45–51: Cooperation Games ◆ 53: The Grouping Game ◆ 57–70: Helping Games

Cooperation Games

Are You Like Me?

Props: Pens and paper for all

Goals
- Becoming integrated into the group
- Enhancing group spirit
- Training self-assessment

How to Play: Each player writes down a list of 5 to 10 qualities that she thinks she has. The game leader can help the players by writing a selection of adjectives on the board.

Each player compares his list with those of the other players. They write down whom they share the most characteristics with. At the end of the game they go and stand by that player.

Examples: Hard-working, lazy, fast, sad, funny, reliable, unreliable, hot-tempered, quiet, tolerant, impatient, patient, friendly, grumpy, tired, argumentative, flexible, punctual.

Variation: One player goes to the center and slowly reads his qualities aloud. When another player hears a word that is on her list, she takes his hand as fast as possible and becomes the next one to read her list of qualities. Again, players who share a quality with her try to be the first ones to touch her hand. That way, the chain becomes longer and longer.

Reflections
- Are the players I share a lot of qualities with also my friends? Is it necessary for a friend to have the same qualities? Can you be friends with someone who is different?
- Why would it be an advantage to have similar qualities? Were the other players in your group surprised by the qualities on your list?

Follow-up Games

13–21: How I Am ♦ 28: Two-Way Interview ♦ 35–39: Perceiving You ♦
46–51: Warming-up Games for the Group ♦ 52: Come into the Circle ♦ 54:
We Are Alike ♦ 85–90: Statue Games

Follow-up Games from *101 Life Skills Games for Children*

27–32: Understanding You ♦ 45–51: Cooperation Games ♦ 53: The
Grouping Game ♦ 94: Fairytale Personalities

We Are Alike

Props: Pens and paper for each group

Goals
- Becoming integrated into the group
- Increasing group spirit
- Learning to cooperate

How to Play: Groups of four players collect as many facts as possible that apply to their group.

Examples: blue eyes, same age, same grade or class, all have siblings, all love sports, all love Bart Simpson, all like French fries, nobody likes doing homework, everybody's shoe size is under 5.

At the end, each group chooses a group name and makes a coat of arms or a logo for the group. Then, each group introduces and explains itself to the larger group.

Variations
- Each group has to design a vacation program that pleases all group members.
- Each group agrees to buy a specific car and house for the group.
- Each group starts a company in which everyone in the group has a job.

Reflections
- Have you learned things about group members that you didn't know before?
- How was the group formed?
- Did somebody in the group take control?
- Who stayed in the background?
- What was your role in the group?

Note: This game is also suitable for warming up. Everyone is usually amazed by all the surprising creative ideas that end up being presented.

Role Play: Members of a small group play the admissions committee of a special school—a school that tries to reduce conflict by accepting only students that fulfill certain criteria. They interview some applicants.

Follow-up Games
53: Are You Like Me? and all of its suggested follow-up games ◆ 55: Birthday Present

Cooperation Games

Birthday Present

Props: Colored pencils or markers and paper. Additional materials may be needed depending on the ideas of each group.

Goals
- Learning to cooperate
- Becoming integrated into the group
- Strengthening relationships

How to Play: Is it anybody's birthday? In groups of four, the players have half an hour to think about a gift for the person whose special day it is. While they're deciding, the birthday child gets to choose a quiet activity outside the room—like drawing or reading. When she comes back in, a representative from each group gives her that group's present.

Examples
- A poem
- A group drawing
- A speech of praise
- A birthday song
- Everybody plays the birthday child's favorite game
- Reading a birthday story aloud

Reflections
- How did you know the gift would please the birthday child?
- Why was the birthday child pleased?

Follow-up Games
54: We Are Alike ◆ 56: Designing a Classroom ◆ 67–73: Relationship Games ◆ 88: Family Statues ◆ 91–92: Simulation Game

Follow-up Games from *101 Life Skills Games for Children*
3: Wishing Cards ◆ 45–51: Cooperation Games ◆ 57–70: Helping Games ◆ 88: Mannequins

Cooperation Games

Designing
a Classroom

Props: Index cards or pieces of paper about 2" x 4"; pens; desks

Goals
- Learning to cooperate
- Learning democratic behavior
- Integrating personal goals with group goals

How to Play: Groups of four are formed. Each group chooses a secretary from among its members. The secretaries each get twenty index cards or 2" x 4" pieces of paper. Now the full group brainstorms on the subject of "school," jotting down terms that go with the subject, things like: notebooks, report card, waste paper basket, hard-working, interesting, teacher, student, studying, cheating, snacking, principal, recess. The secretaries of each group write down each term on a separate index card. The suggestions of the players shouldn't come any faster than the secretaries can write them down.

When they have collected 20 terms, each small group starts furnishing their classroom, using a desk as the floor plan. The furniture (tables, book cases, partitions, board) are the cards that have been written on. They are arranged on the floor plan. Cards with terms that the groups do not want to dedicate any space to go into the trash. When arranging the furniture, there are interesting choices to make: whether word groups are arranged as desk groups, which cards are close to the center, which ones are farthest from the center, and which are at the corners. Are the desks in rows, in a U-shape, in groups, or jumbled? Unusual arrangements of furniture are also possible.

At the end of the furnishing process, which can last 15 to 30 minutes, the individual groups present their classrooms to each other. They explain why they have chosen their arrangement, why they have put various terms next to each other, and so forth.

Reflections
- Were there strong differences of opinion in your group? Was there something everyone agreed on?

- What could really be arranged differently in your classroom?
- How actively did you participate in your own group's discussion?
- Were your ideas taken seriously enough?
- Why will some of these ideas never be put into practice?

Follow-up Games

33: Favorite Place ◆ 40–45: Working with You ◆ 55: Birthday Present ◆ 57: Designing an Apartment ◆ 58: Designing a City ◆ 59: Space Expedition ◆ 91–92: Simulation Games

Follow-up Games from *101 Life Skills Games for Children*

8: Observing the Room ◆ 45–51: Cooperation Games ◆ 90: Class Picture

Designing an Apartment

Props: Index cards or pieces of paper about 2" x 4"; pens; desks

Goals

- Learning to cooperate
- Practicing democratic behavior
- Integrating personal goals with group goals

How to Play: This is played like Game #56. The full group brainstorms on the subject of "home," listing terms that go with the subject. For example: dog, refrigerator, potted plants, beds, brother, television, closet, cookie jar, father, telephone, pantry, stereo, mother. The secretaries of each group write down each term on a separate card. The suggestions of the players shouldn't come any faster than the secretaries can write them down.

When they have collected 20 terms, each small group starts furnishing their apartment, using a desk as the floor plan. Rooms of the apartment can be defined by putting strips of masking tape where the walls would be. The furniture (beds, tables) are the cards that have been written on. They are arranged on the floor plan. Cards with terms that the groups decide not to dedicate any space to go into the wastebasket. When arranging the furniture, it is important to consider which words are arranged as groups, and which are separate even if they're in the same room.

At the end of the furnishing process, which can last 15 to 30 minutes, the groups show their apartments to each other. They explain why they have chosen their particular arrangement and why they have grouped certain terms together. They also explain the housewarming party they would like to have.

Reflections and Follow-up Games

See all the reflections and follow-up games for Game #56.

Designing a City

Props: Index cards or pieces of paper about 2" x 4"; pens; desks

Goals

- Learning to cooperate
- Learning democratic behavior
- Integrating personal goals with group goals

How to Play: This is played like Games #56 and #57. The full group brain-storms on the subject of "city," listing relevant terms. For example: park, fire station, newspaper office, bowling alley, peaceful, school, hardware store, traffic, shopping mall, skate park, video arcade, movie theater. The secre-taries of each group write down each term on a separate card.

When they have collected 20 terms, each small group starts designing their city, using a desk as the city plan. The buildings or public facilities (fire station, shopping mall) are the cards that have been written on. They are arranged on the city plan. Cards with terms that the groups do not want to dedicate any space to go into the bin. When designing the city, it is also im-portant to consider which word groups (buildings) should be arranged to-gether, which cards are close to the center, which ones are farthest from the center, and which are at the corners. Unusual arrangements are also possible.

Allow the groups at least 15 to 30 minutes to complete their cities. Once they are finished, the groups present their cities to each other: They explain why they have chosen their particular arrangement, why they have put this building next to that one, and why they tossed out certain words.

Reflections and Follow-up Games

See all the reflections and follow-up games for Game #56.

Space Expedition

Props: Chairs or benches

Goals
- Integrating into the group
- Determining positions
- Enlisting people in one's ideas
- Developing cooperation

How to Play: The players form groups of six to eight people. Each group arranges seats in a spaceship that will be flying to a distant planet for a year. All possible jobs can be assigned: captain, pilot, copilot, engineer, cook, radio operator, historian, and so forth.

Once all positions have been determined, the group gets a few problems that they have to solve in a discussion:

1. An alien spaceship is on the attack. Only a skilful and brave emergency squad can save the spaceship from destruction.
2. Several engines are failing. Part of the crew has to transfer to the smaller auxiliary spaceship. Chances of survival are small.
3. The captain has developed a mysterious mental illness. He behaves in a way that is perilous for the whole crew.
4. An unknown planet is in sight. Nobody knows anything about it. They need supplies. Should they land?
5. An alien spaceship with a potent magnetic field has brought the spaceship under its control. It sends a message: Surrender one crew member, and the rest of you can escape! What now?

Each group now has to spontaneously solve another problem in a role game. The problem is similar to the ones discussed before.

1. The spaceship has been caught by a UFO and is held by its tentacles. Some crew members have to leave the spaceship to detach the tentacles. These brave people might not survive.

2. For mysterious reasons, part of the food in the spaceship has become inedible. There isn't going to be enough for everybody, so part of the crew has to be dropped off on an unfamiliar planet and picked up again on the ship's way back, when they have more supplies.
3. It is unclear how much longer the spaceship will be technically operational. The occupants of the extra-terrestrial spaceship are offering the crew a transfer to their spaceship.
4. The space radio communication system broadcasts that 90 percent of all space food is contaminated. Has the virus, which has an immediate lethal effect, also attacked our spaceship? Will the whole crew have to starve to death? If one person tests the food pill, they'll know.

Reflections
- Who is happy or unhappy with the result?
- If you were to play this game again, would anybody prefer to have a different role?
- Both active and observing group members participate in the reflective conversation.

Follow-up Games
20: Pieces of Personality ◆ 40–45: Working with You ◆ 56: Designing a Classroom ◆ 67–73: Relationship Games ◆ 91–92: Simulation Games ◆ 93–101: Social Role-Play Games

Follow-up Games from *101 Life Skills Games for Children*
33–40: Working with You ◆ 45–51: Cooperation Games ◆ 69: Carrying Contest

Seeing with Your Fingertips

Props: Four pairs of related objects

Goals
- Integrating new members to the group
- Training tactile perception
- Understanding disability

How to Play: This game is very suitable for introducing and integrating a new student, but it can also be played even if there isn't a new student. The newcomer is blindfolded while other players choose four pairs of related objects and scatter them on a rug. The newcomer tries to figure out what they are by touch. He arranges them in pairs, names them, and tries to guess a collective term for them.

Example: Two pencils, two erasers, two pencil sharpeners, and two ball-point pens (in this case, the collective term might be "school supplies").

Variations
- Items with different textures (rough, smooth, sandpapery)
- Wooden letters in pairs
- Groups of wooden letters (with straight lines; with round ones; with mixed)
- Divide objects into two piles: school supplies and toys
- Ordering wooden sticks, stones, or buttons by size and weight
- "What's Missing?" One player removes an object. By touch, the blind player finds out what is missing.

Reflection: Would a visually impaired person be better at this game? If so, then being able to see is a handicap!

Follow-up Games
48: Lost in the Dark Woods ◆ 61: The Blind Person and the Movie

Follow-up Games from *101 Life Skills Games for Children*
27–32: Understanding You ◆ 34: Helping Hands ◆ 45–51: Cooperation
Games ◆ 57–70: Helping Games

The Blind Person and the Movie

Props: A movie, and a way to show it; blindfolds for at least half of the group

Goals
- Experiencing what it is like to have a disability
- Helping
- Training acoustic perception

How to Play: The basis of this game is a short movie (10–20 minutes). One group of players listens to the movie blindfolded, and the other watches it the usual way. Two players wait outside the room.

After the movie, the blindfolded players remove their blindfolds and the two outside people come back in. The group of blindfolded players tells the two outside players about the movie. The other group fills in the gaps, providing the information the first group missed.

Reflections

- What are the differences between the hearing-and-seeing experience and just hearing?
- What limitations does a visually impaired person have in narrating what she has experienced?
- What are some of the things in the environment that a blind person would not know about unless someone else described them?

Follow-up Games

31: Rumor Factory ◆ 49: Stumbling over Roots ◆ 60: Seeing with Your Fingertips ◆ 62: Blindness in Everyday Life

Follow-up Games from *101 Life Skills Games for Children*

6–7: What I Can Do ◆ 8–19: What I Observe ◆ 27–32: Understanding You ◆ 34: Helping Hands ◆ 45–51: Cooperation Games ◆ 57–70: Helping Games

Integration Games

Blindness in Everyday Life

Props: Chairs and tables; various household implements; bottles of water; some bread or crackers

Goals
- Experiencing what it is like to have a disability
- Training tactile perception
- Helping

How to Play: The group splits into pairs. In each pair is a "blind" person and a "narrator" who helps him. Each narrator has a piece of paper with the day's routine. Sentence by sentence she reads the routine to the blind person who pantomimes the actions. The narrator has to make sure that "her" blind person does not hurt himself.

Example: The day's routine: Max (Molly), who is blind or partially sighted, is lying in bed (tables, chairs, benches put together). He rolls from one side to the other. The alarm clock goes off. Max sits up, climbs out of the bed, and looks for his slippers. He looks for the bathroom door, opens it, and looks for the sink. He washes and dries himself. Then he goes back into the bedroom.

He puts on pants and a shirt, buttons everything up, and puts on his shoes. The shoelaces have to be tied tightly so he won't trip. Somewhere on the coat rack next to the door are Max's hat and umbrella. Now Max walks down the stairs to the next floor. He opens the window and determines what the weather is like today. He's no longer in the mood for a walk. He goes back to his room.

On the sideboard, there is a soup bowl, a plate, silverware, a coffee cup, and a water bottle. Now Max scoops soup (actually water) from the pot into the soup bowl. When he's finished eating, he takes a piece of meat (actually bread or a cracker) from the pan, puts it on the plate, and eats it with fork and knife. He drinks "juice" that he has poured from the water bottle into the cup. When he is finished, he carries the dishes to the sink to rinse and dry them. Then he puts everything back on the sideboard. He goes to the toy shelf and plays for a while (there is a selection of real toys on the shelves. Then he reads a bit in Braille before he lies down for his afternoon nap (on the Braille sheet, touchable letters can be attached that say, "You did a great job, Max."

Note: This is not a game for everyone to play at the same time. It can be a special assignment that players tackle with their partners at different times throughout the week. Then, at the end of the week or month, several sets of partners can report back to the group on their experiences. The blind person can end the game at any point it gets exhausting.

Reflections
- What was particularly difficult?
- Why did you interrupt the game?
- Did you have to peek?
- How was it to play, eat, put on clothes, climb stairs without being able to see?
- Could you do these activities without help?
- How could you practice these activities?

Follow-up Games
61: The Blind Person and the Movie ◆ 63: The Blind Group

Integration Games

The Blind Group

Goals
- Experiencing what it is like to have a disability
- Training acoustic perception

How to Play: The game leader positions up to five players at different places around the room. Sitting on the floor, eyes closed, they call out each other's names in turn, and respond by saying "I'm here!" This way, each player knows roughly where the others are sitting. One of the "blind" players, who has been chosen by the game leader, gets up and carefully walks to the next player, touches him and says his name. If the name is correct, that player gets up, shakes hands with the first player, and together they look for the next person sitting on the floor. The game continues until all players form a line. If a player says a wrong name, she has to first look for another blind player. The blind players who are walking can discuss with each other who the person sitting on the floor might be, but the ones still sitting must keep silent.

Variation: After the names have been called out, helpers lead all blind players to the side of the room, where they open their eyes. One of them puts the players back to the place where she thought they had been sitting.

Role Plays
- 4 blind children playing games (ball games, board games, building blocks) with and without supervision
- 4 blind and 2 sighted children playing
- 2 blind and 2 sighted children playing
- The day our blind classmate was taunted by a stranger
- I'm telling my friend about our new blind classmate

Follow-up Games
All follow-up games suggested for 61: The Blind Person and the Movie ◆ 62: Blindness in Everyday Life ◆ 64: Blind Pool

Blind Pool

Goals
- Integration
- Protecting
- Helping
- Cooperating
- Developing trust

How to Play: A volunteer is standing at the center of a circle formed by the other players. The volunteer starts walking "blindly" in one direction. When she comes within half a yard of a player, he warns her against bumping into him by shouting "(Name), watch out!" The blind player changes direction and keeps walking until the next player warns her.

Variations
- When the blind player is in danger of bumping into the circle, she is called and warned from behind.
- The blind player walks between a double line of players. The alley is about two yards wide and can have turns.
- The players form a line that represents a path that meanders through the room. The other players lead her along the path by whispering her name.

Tips
- Not all children like to play a blind person.
- Not all children like to stand "blind" in the middle while the other players have their eyes open. They feel awkward being watched. That is especially the case for children that are new in the group or class.

Reflections
- Were you afraid of touching anyone?
- What was it like to hear your name as a blind person?
- Were you able to orient yourself?

Role Plays

- A blind student is to be integrated into the class. Today he enters the classroom for the first time. Other students play tricks on the blind classmate.
- The morning my mother woke me up and I couldn't see anything any more.
- After a six-month stay at the hospital following a severe accident, I'm back home. The doorbell rings. I open the door. My old friends have come to pick me up to play with them for the first time again.

Follow-up Games

63: The Blind Group ◆ 65: Hearing Nothing

Hearing Nothing

Props: Earplugs and bandannas for all

Goals
- Experiencing what it is like to have a disability
- Helping
- Cooperating
- Developing trust
- Communicating nonverbally

How to Play: The players put earplugs into their ears and wrap bandannas around their heads. They engage in various games and activities to experience what it's like to be deaf. Some possibilities for communication are the following:
- Pantomime
- Sign language and finger letters
- Written communication

Note: Socially, deaf people are sometimes far more isolated than blind people. They suffer from the fact that they can communicate with other people better than other people can communicate with them. No matter how hard deaf people try, other people often misunderstand them or get impatient. Understanding this isolation and trying to have patience in communicating with deaf people can be the main objectives of exercises and games in this area with nonhandicapped children.

Follow-up Games
64: Blind Pool ◆ 66: Disability of the Extremities

Follow-up Games from *101 Life Skills Games for Children*
8–19: What I Observe ◆ 78: Peace Language ◆ 97–101: Pantomime Play

Disability of the Extremities

Props: Balloons

Goals
- Experiencing what it is like to have a diability
- Helping
- Learning to deal with disabilities

How to Play: During the next half hour, six to eight players stick balloons between their knees while the activities of the class go on as usual. The "disabled" and the "nondisabled" report afterward how the game went for them.

Variation: For a quarter of the players, index finger, middle finger, and ring finger are tied together. Together with the "nondisabled" ones, they play games in which they need to use their hands.

Follow-up Games
1–10: What I'm Feeling ♦ 40–45: Working with You ♦ 49: Stumbling over Roots ♦ 64: Blind Pool ♦ 65: Hearing Nothing

Follow-up Games from *101 Life Skills Games for Children*
31: You Move Me ♦ 33–40: Working with You ♦ 45–51: Cooperation Games

Group-net

Goals
- Exploring connections and relationships in the group
- Recognizing commonalities
- Integrating into the group
- Strengthening group spirit
- Showing affection

How to Play: The group sits in a circle. One player goes to the center. Another player joins her, puts his hand on her shoulder and says what connects him with the first player. A third player joins them, then a fourth, until all players are in the "group-net." Some players have connections to several players, which they express verbally and visually by putting their hands on as many shoulders as they can reach.

Example
First player: "My name is Sarah."
Second player (Michael): "I live on the same street as Sarah."
Third player (Samantha): "During recess I played tag with Sarah." (Positions herself next to Sarah.)
Fourth player (Joshua): "My birthday is on the same day as Michael's." (Positions himself next to Michael.)
Fifth player (Jessica): "Michael, Joshua, and I often play with each other." (Puts one hand each on Michael and Joshua.)

Note: This game can be played several times. The group-net will look different every time. If they play more than once, the players can determine whether they prefer to be in the middle of the group or not.

Follow-up Games
20: Pieces of Personality ◆ 27: Meet Me Halfway ◆ 35–39: Perceiving You ◆ 46–51: Warming-up Games for the Group ◆ 52: Come into the Circle ◆ 55: Birthday Present ◆ 85–90: Statue and Sculpting Games

Follow-up Games from *101 Life Skills Games for Children*
21: Crossword Puzzle Names ◆ 23: Autograph Book ◆ 27: I Met My Match ◆ 33–40: Working with You ◆ 41–44: Warming-up Games for the Group ◆ 50: Tug of War

Birthday Party

Goals

- Exploring connections and relationships in the group
- Dealing with invitations (and not being invited)
- Strengthening group spirit
- Integrating into the group
- Showing affection

How to Play: As in Group-net (Game #67), one player starts the game by going to the center of the circle. Perhaps it's this player's birthday today? She calls other players into the center, stating a reason and thereby inviting them to a party. An invited player joins the players standing at the center. They can choose their own spot. The game continues until all players are invited to the party.

Examples

- "Samantha, I'm inviting you to my party because you are my best friend."
- "Sarah, I'm inviting you because you shared your snack with me yesterday."

Follow-up Games

67: Group-net ◆ 69: My Place in the Group

My Place in the Group

Props: Chairs

Goals
- Making connections and relationships in the group visible
- Dealing with marginalized groups and integrating them
- Showing affection and rejection
- Strengthening group spirit

How to Play: All players are standing along the sides of the room. One by one, they walk into the center of the room, take a chair, and sit down where they feel comfortable. If another player puts their chair close by, they can move toward or away from them. There is no talking during this game.

Note: It's better to play this game only with experienced game players and after other group-forming activities. It can be repeated several times. The game leader can determine who will go after whom by asking the players to form a circle. After the game, it's important to get together in a circle and talk about dislikes that have become evident. Here, dislikes and loners and outsiders can be recognized and dealt with. In addition to talking about it, Integration Games, Cooperation Games, and You Games can help improve the group situation.

In the conversation, special attention needs to be given to players who were unhappy with the result of the game. Likewise, the observations of players who are standing on the sides are important. Since the game is a "snapshot" of the group situation, it can have a different result the second time it is played. Groupdynamic processes that have been initiated by the conversation and other games that have been played in the meantime may be integrated there.

Reflections
- Why did you move away or closer?
- Did someone become an outsider?

- Did the game show you who is actually the center of attention in everyday life? What is connected with that?
- What traits does the person have who is at the center of attention?
- How could you get the players who remain standing on the sides to be more involved? Do we want to include them? Do they want to be included?
- In which situation in everyday life have you felt like the center of attention or an outsider? Did it make you feel comfortable or uncomfortable? Did the situation change? How?
- Which groups in your neighborhood may be considered "outsiders"? What is your attitude toward them?
- Do you know someone who has a dislike for marginalized groups? What effect does it have?

Role Plays
- A disagreeable person is sitting at the restaurant table next to you.
- A conflict takes place in a bus or on the subway.
- I don't want to sit next to this person any more!

Follow-up Games
1: A Picture of My Mood ◆ 20: Pieces of Personality ◆ 31: Rumor Factory ◆ 45: Accidental Partners ◆ 52–59: Cooperation Games ◆ 60–66: Integration Games ◆ 68: Birthday Party ◆ 70: Spider Web ◆ 77: Circle of Threat ◆ 81: Gauntlet ◆ 90: Freeze Frame

Follow-up Games from *101 Life Skills Games for Children*
20–26: Getting to Know You ◆ 27–32: Understanding You ◆ 43: Greeting Game ◆ 45–51: Cooperation Games ◆ 52–56: Integration Games ◆ 57–70: Helping Games ◆ 72: Tug of War II ◆ 77: Frontline ◆ 79: Rumors

Spider Web

Props: At least one large ball of yarn

Goals
- Making connections
- Making connections in the group visible
- Integrating into the group

How to Play: In this well-known game that many children around the world like to play, a ball of yarn is unwound as it is rolled from one player to the next in a circle. The player who gets it holds the yarn tight and rolls the ball to another player, maybe shouting out the name of the person who's supposed to get it. The ball of wool can land at the same player several times, which can indicate a lot of connections with other players.

Afterward, the woolen thread net can be carried through the room. The threads should be as tight as possible. Players can overcome obstacles (tables, chairs, etc.). The game has now become a cooperation game.

Variation: The game can be played with several balls of wool of different colors at the same time.

Follow-up Games
69: My Place in the Group and all of its suggested follow-up games ◆ 71: Name Fields

Name Fields

Props: Pens and oversized paper; a table

Goals
- Making connections and relationships in the group visible

How to Play: Each player writes her name on a large sheet of paper, circles it, and puts the sheet on a table. Then all players go from sheet to sheet and add their names. When doing so, they make sure that the distance from their own name to the encircled name reflects their relationship to that person, and also to the other people who have added their names on the sheet.

In the end, players can report to the group what they think of their name field.

Note: The disadvantage of this game is that the position of the name cannot be changed after the event. Moving away from the names that have been added is not possible. For more tips and reflections see My Place in the Group (Game #69).

Follow-up Games
All follow-up games suggested for 69: My Place in the Group ◆ 70: Spider Web ◆ 72: Stone Field

Stone Field

Props: One or more bags of colored stones, depending on group size

Goal: Making connections and relationships in the group visible

How to Play: The group sits in a circle, and the group leader passes around a bag of colored stones. Each player looks for a stone they like. A square cloth about 2 yards across is laid on the floor at the center of the circle. One by one, all the players lay their stones on the cloth. Once all the stones have been laid, their positions can be changed in a second and third round. Stone clusters will develop. Some stones are surrounded by a lot of other stones, some prefer to be by themselves, some like to be at the margin of a stone group, some like to be at the edge of the cloth, others in the middle.

Note: Since it could get confusing if there are too many different colors of stones, the players can be divided into two groups or more. Players can also be regrouped after they have played a round, and see what their relationships are with the other players. For more tips and reflections see My Place in the Group (Game #69).

Follow-up Games
All follow-up games suggested for 69: My Place in the Group ◆ 71: Name Fields ◆ 73: In Orbit

In Orbit

Props: Pens and index cards or slips of paper; glue; oversized paper

Goal: Demonstrating friendship preferences

How to Play: The group leader counts the number of people in the group, and then each player writes his name on that many index cards or slips of paper and puts these on their chair. Now everybody walks around and gets a card or slip from each chair so they have one from each group member. They then get a large sheet of paper and glue their own names at the center of the sheet and group the other names around them as they like.

When everyone is done, they visit each other's sheets to see their groupings and the place they have on the posters of the other players.

Note: It makes sense to play this game in a group that is well acquainted with each other. For more tips and reflections see My Place in the Group (Game #69).

Follow-up Games
All follow-up games suggested for 69: My Place in the Group ◆ 72: Stone Field

Follow-up Games from *101 Life Skills Games for Children*
21: Crossword Puzzle Names ◆ 23: Autograph Book

Something Nice

Props: Pens, slips of paper, and a box to draw them out of

Goals
- Controlling aggressive feelings
- Learning sympathy
- Giving and accepting gifts

How to Play: Each player writes three tasks on separate slips of paper. The tasks are requests for other players to do something nice. All the slips are shuffled and put in a big box. Each player picks a slip and does the task written on it. He then replaces the slip in the box and draws a new one.

Examples
"Look for a flower for Sarah."
"Give a classmate a compliment!"
"Promise something nice to Jacob."
"Piggyback a classmate to a nice spot in the room!"

Variations
- Small groups write the slips and then make them available to the entire group. Writing them in groups will make it more likely that the tasks can actually be accomplished, because there is bound to be some discussion.
- Sitting in a circle, all players say what nice things they would wish for themselves. Then the slips are written.

Reflections
- Was there a task that was difficult or unpleasant to fulfill? Did that make it even more satisfying as a favor to do for someone?
- What kinds of tasks did you like to fulfill? Which ones were people particularly grateful for?

Role Plays

- A stranger says, "May I help you?"
- Somebody gives you a gift that does not please you.
- Somebody gives you a compliment that you perceive as flattery.
- You would like to give something nice to your grandma but you don't know what would make her happy.
- You have a nice gift for your teacher, but because you don't know if she'll appreciate it you hesitate to give it to her.

Follow-up Games

20: Pieces of Personality ◆ 26: Hello, Goodbye ◆ 34: Picture Present ◆ 35–39: Perceiving You ◆ 46: Punctuation Mark ◆ 47: Name Chain ◆ 68: Birthday Party ◆ 75: President of Praise

Follow-up Games from *101 Life Skills Games for Children*

1–5: What I Like ◆ 18: Collecting Sound Qualities ◆ 26: The Seat on My Right Is Empty (with a Twist) ◆ 33–40: Working with You ◆ 41–44: Warming-up Games for the Group ◆ 45–51: Cooperation Games ◆ 58: The Comforter Game ◆ 62: The Emergency Kit ◆ 68: Moving Help ◆ 70: First Day at School

75

President of Praise

Goals
- Debating fairly
- Avoiding verbal aggressiveness
- Dealing with competition

How to Play: Everyone in class, or selected candidates, try to get elected president. Here's how it works: Two at a time, in two-minute campaign speeches, they praise their opponent to the skies. The class votes on each pair of candidates. The candidate who makes the best speech about the other candidate becomes the nominee. Now the nominees have a run-off election, again pairing off. Another vote is taken. This continues until only one candidate is left. He is the President of Praise!

Variation: One candidate's job is to be as aggressive as possible. She condemns the other candidate, accusing him of corruption, irresponsibility, and incompetence, while the other one conciliates, is friendly, and praises the opponent.

Reflections
- How does it feel to be praised to the skies?
- Would you like to make people feel like that all the time?

Role Plays
- The father praises his child to the teacher while the child is present. The teacher finds the praise a bit exaggerated.
- The teacher complains to the parents about their child. The parents defend their child.
- At home, the child complains about the teacher, tearing her to shreds. The parents try to show that the teacher has the student's best interests in mind.
- Several speakers campaign for their own election or for the election of the candidate of their choice.

Follow-up Games

13–21: How I Am ◆ 74: Something Nice ◆ 76: Playing Politics ◆ 80: Face-off ◆ 91–92: Simulation Game ◆ 93–101: Social Role-Play Games

Follow-up Games from *101 Life Skills Games for Children*

20–26: Getting to Know You ◆ 54: Hot Seat ◆ 71–83: Aggression Games

76

Playing Politics

Props: Pens and paper

Goals
- Learning about politics and citizenship
- Forming groups with similar ideals
- Convincing, enlisting

How to Play: The players brainstorm on the topic of election promises. Players make election promises, which a campaign volunteer writes on the board.

Now each player writes on a piece of paper the three promises that would appeal most to them as voters. They compose short election speeches for each election promise (three sentences per promise, a total of nine sentences). Now two volunteers play the politicians and read their own election speeches to everyone else.

During their speeches, as soon as one of the "politicians" has read a promise that corresponds to one of the three the other players have written on their own piece a paper, those players go and join this politician. The players that haven't been won over by a politician look for like-minded players (i.e., players that share a similar or identical promise). Some players will still not be chosen. They are the undecided voters. They may vote for the personality of the politician instead, but they can also choose not to vote or to caste an invalid ballot. These voters now have a discussion, in which the two politicians and their supporters also participate. Then they come to a decision. Which politician has won the election?

Role Plays
- Mayoral election
- Election of class president

Follow-up Games
11–12: What I'm Thinking ◆ 13: Missing Person ◆ 28: Two-Way Interview

◆ 30: Heads Are Truthful, Tails Lie ◆ 31: Rumor Factory ◆ 35–39: Perceiving You ◆ 67–73: Relationship Games ◆ 75: President of Praise ◆ 77: Circle of Threat ◆ 91–92: Simulation Game ◆ 96: Interview

Follow-up Games from *101 Life Skills Games for Children*
6–7: What I Can Do ◆ 27–32: Understanding You ◆ 50: Tug of War ◆ 71–83: Aggression Games

Circle of Threat

Goals
- Dealing with aggression
- Reducing and abstaining from aggression
- Dealing with fear

How to Play: A volunteer goes to the center of the circle. The other players threaten him with menacing gestures. The volunteer thinks of and suddenly does something that makes everyone lighten up.

Note: Timid or aggressive players should not play the volunteer.

Reflections
- Did you feel like crawling away and hiding in a corner? Did you feel like exploding and getting nasty?
- Are there people who make you feel threatened?
- Are there groups of people you feel threatened by?

Role Plays
- You come home with a bad grade. The whole family attacks you.
- A classmate is injured in a brawl. You were part of it. The principal and teacher are blaming you.
- The police have arrested you. They are interrogating you. You are suspected of being a notorious bank robber.
- You are a tourist. In a restaurant full of locals, people start whispering. Everybody looks at you. Some people stand up.

Follow-up Games
1–10: What I'm Feeling ◆ 31: Rumor Factory ◆ 50: Through the Thicket ◆ 64: Blind Pool ◆ 69: My Place in the Group ◆ 76: Playing Politics ◆ 78: Jostle

Follow-up Games from *101 Life Skills Games for Children*
32: When It Rains, It Pours ◆ 45–51: Cooperation Games ◆ 61: Cry for Help ◆ 67: Crocodile Tears ◆ 71–83: Aggression Games

Jostle

Goal
- Understanding fear of aggression

How to Play: All players spread out and position themselves around the room, leaving only about half a yard between each other. A volunteer goes to one side of the room and tries to get through to the other side by walking through the crowd. As she walks, the other players move closer together to make her passage more and more difficult. These players cannot push, grab, or hold her, and she can push just enough to make her way through. In this game, players are not allowed to run, only walk.

Variation: Two players are walking closely side by side. They want to get to the other side of the room. The crowd tries to push them apart.

Reflections
- What feelings did you have when you were hassled?
- Was it fear, anger, or aggressiveness?
- Were you thinking of giving up your goal?
- What situations in everyday life are similar?
- How were you able to help yourself?

Role Plays
- Jostling on the bus
- Jostling at school
- Trying to cross the street in heavy traffic

Follow-up Games
77: Circle of Threat ◆ 79: War Dance

War Dance

Goals
- Reducing aggression
- Tolerating aggression
- Getting to know forms of aggression

How to Play: In small groups of six to eight, players rehearse war dances. Drumming or a tape with rhythmical music can be the background music. Each group presents their dance with the other groups watching. They try to find out what form of aggression (which kind of dance) it is.

Examples
- A dance for preparing mentally, boosting courage, and generally getting people in a fighting mood before a battle.
- A dance for scaring away the enemy before fighting begins.
- A dance for supporting your own warriors when the battle is taking place.

Variation: The dancers move around the other players, who are sitting on the floor in the middle of the room.

Reflections
- What mood did the dancing evoke in you?
- What effect did the dancing have on the group?

Role Plays
- At the totem pole
- The day the god of war appeared to the warriors.

Follow-up Games
1–10: What I'm Feeling ◆ 78: Jostle ◆ 80: Face-off ◆ 85–90: Statue and Sculpting Games

Follow-up Games from *101 Life Skills Games for Children*
71–83: Aggression Games

Aggression Games

Face-off

Props: Aggression Cards (see the Master Sheet that follows the game)

Goals
- Seeing through aggressive behavior
- Practicing visual perception

How to Play: Two prehistoric cave people encounter each other in a hostile way. Belonging to two different tribes, they don't share the same language. Both feel they have to stand up for themselves against the other. They try to make the other one retreat with noises, facial expressions, and gestures. Their behavior is determined by an aggression card, which they draw from a pack and don't let anyone else see.

After a few minutes, at a signal from the game leader, both players withdraw. With the help of players in the audience, each player tries to guess what was written on her opponent's card.

Examples
- "Shake a spear or your fists and look angry."
- "Pound your chest and roar like a gorilla!"

Reflections
- How can I intimidate or scare someone?
- Is intimidation the same as an actual attack?
- Who has intimidated you in everyday life?
- What "modern" means are there for intimidating, in addition to facial expressions, gestures, and language?
- Name some animals that show intimidating behaviors.

Role Plays
- Two contemporary enemies tangle with each other.
- There would have been a fight if the teacher hadn't intervened.

Follow-up Games
4: Body Language Spells Your Mood ◆ 23: What's My Name ◆ 36: Spy ◆

54: We Are Alike ◆ 79: War Dance ◆ 81: Gauntlet ◆ 85–90: Statue and Sculpting Games ◆ 93–101: Social Role-Play Games

Follow-up Games from *101 Life Skills Games for Children*
28: You Sculpt Me ◆ 29: You Reflect Me ◆ 44: Good Morning! ◆ 60: Friendly Exam ◆ 71–83: Aggression Games ◆ 84–92: Statue and Sculpting Games ◆ 97–101: Pantomime Play

Master Sheet for Face-off

Don't get too close to me!	I'm the strongest! This is my territory!	Get lost; otherwise you'll be in trouble!
I'm tall and handsome.	I can be really dangerous. Another word, and I'll knock you out!	I have already finished off a lot of enemies.
Don't make me angry!	I don't care about you.	I'll beat you up.
I find you pathetic and ridiculous.	Look what weapons I have!	My friends and helpers are close by here.
I'm sorry for you.	You are so inferior to me.	I'm only acting as if I'm afraid of you.

Gauntlet

Goals
- Tolerating aggression and provocation
- Understanding outsiders
- Understanding loneliness in a crowd

How to Play: Players are divided into two groups. One group forms two lines that get closer at one end like a funnel. The other group has to enter and walk through this funnel one by one. With gestures, facial expressions, and shouts, the players forming the gauntlet try to induce various feelings in the players walking through: amusement, anger, fear, or joy.

Variations
- Walking blind through the gauntlet
- Walking though the gauntlet laughing, singing, or shouting
- Walking through the gauntlet in pairs
- Running, jumping, dancing through
- Laughing at the players in line, shouting at them or making threatening gestures
- Talking to the players in a calming way
- Talking to oneself

Reflection: Have you ever been in a situation in which you felt you were treated unpleasantly as an outsider? Do you have a "trick" for handling such situations?

Role Play: A new student enters the school. Everybody starts whispering, wondering where she's from, looking her over, and testing her.

Follow-up Games
1–10: What I'm Feeling ◆ 80: Face-off ◆ 82: Security Guard

Follow-up Games from *101 Life Skills Games for Children*
45–51: Cooperation Games ◆ 57–70: Helping Games ◆ 71–83: Aggression Games

82

Aggression Games

Security Guard

Props: Building blocks

Goals
- Dealing with stealing
- Dealing with mistrust
- Training visual perception
- Dealing with the fear of getting caught

How to Play: Scattered around the room are colorful building blocks, at least three times as many as there are players. The game leader chooses one player as a security guard by tapping him on the shoulder while everyone's eyes are closed. Then all the players open their eyes and walk around the room trying to steal the blocks. The security guard can't possibly catch all the thieves at once, but he gets them one by one by telling each thief what his loot looks like, where he has stashed it away, or what hand he's hiding it in. Thieves who have been found out drop out of the game.

The security guard's identity is revealed as soon as he catches the first thief, but that is okay—it'll be just as hard for the other thieves to achieve their goal, which is to collect three blocks without getting caught. The first to do that shouts: "You're fired!" Another player is chosen to be the new security guard in the next round.

Reflections
- Was it stressful for you to play the security guard or a thief?
- Were you afraid of being caught as a thief?
- What happens to shoplifters in everyday life?
- What might the reasons be why some customers steal?
- What influence can you have on someone who steals?

Notes
- In this game, reflection is particularly important. Adolescents often shoplift. Many of them are surprised by the unpleasant consequences. The role-play is designed to illustrate this problem.

- This game is deliberately meant to be difficult for the security guard. That way he can experience the feelings of someone, such as a shop owner, who has to deal with people who may try to steal from her.

Role Plays

- Caught shoplifting in the department store!
- Son, our neighbor told me she saw you stealing in the department store!
- Mother: "Where did you get this computer game from? You didn't steal it, did you?"
- Steve boasts in front of his friends, "Every time I go to the store, I rip something off!"

- Martina says to her friends, "If you're not a coward, you'll take something from the cosmetics department!"
- If you don't lend me five dollars, I'll tell the teacher I saw you stealing something from her desk!"

Follow-up Games

1–10: What I'm Feeling ◆ 36: Spy ◆ 81: Gauntlet ◆ 83: Agent Game

Follow-up Games from *101 Life Skills Games for Children*

8–19: What I Observe ◆ 71–83: Aggression Games

83

Aggression Games

Agent Game

Props: Slips of paper prepared in advance by the game leader

Goals
- Dealing with mistrust
- Dealing with the fear of being found out
- Showing solidarity

How to Play: In this game there is a spy and about six to eight informants. The rest of the players are agents who have to find and arrest the spy. Before these roles are determined, all players have to close their eyes. The game leader inconspicuously hands one player a slip of paper with the word "spy" written on it. Each informant is handed a slip of paper with a brief description of the spy, for example: blue eyes, white sneakers, blond hair, pants, very tall. The agents also get slips that simply say "agent."

All players open their eyes and read their slips carefully, then hide them in their pockets and close their eyes again. Now the game leader calls out: "Open your eyes! Look for the spy!" All players get up, go to the other players and ask each of them one question at a time, for example, "What color is the spy's shirt?" Usually they'll get the answer, "I don't know," since only the informants have a piece of information. The informants can only pass on the information on their slip of paper if someone asks them the right question (or questions, if the informant has gathered more information). The spy doesn't betray himself and answers all questions with "I don't know." No players are allowed to ask about each other's identities. The agent who thinks she has identified the spy quietly asks another player to be her partner. They approach the alleged spy together and say, "You are under arrest!" If they are wrong, they are out of the game.

Reflections
- In this game, players have to rely on the cooperation of the others even though they don't trust them. Is it a relief to find allies after a while?
- What was exciting for the spy?

- What would a real spy do differently?
- Which role would suit you best?

Role Play: Which student has gotten us in trouble with the teacher?

Follow-up Games
82: Security Guard and all of its suggested follow-up games ◆ 84: Chase

Chase

Goals
- Dealing with fear and aggression
- Practicing consideration and not being aggressive

How to Play: In this game, players are both "chasers" trying to catch a victim and victims who are chased by another player. To begin, all the players walk around the room. As they walk, each player silently chooses another player—any other player—to be her victim and starts staring at him. At the same time, another player may choose her as his victim. After a while, most of the players will become aware of who is chasing them.

At a signal from the game leader, the players run and try to catch their victims before they are caught themselves. The ones who get caught freeze. Many players will get caught before they catch their own victims.

Variation: There are two groups. Group A starts out as pursuers. Players from Group A each stare at a player from Group B as they walk around. Players from Group B keep their eyes on their pursuers so they can escape in time. Players who get caught continue walking because pretty soon, at a signal from the game leader, the players from Group B become the pursuers.

Note: The game leader has to advise players not to bump into each other. A less dangerous version would be to play the game on all fours, like animals chasing each other.

Reflections
- Have you ever felt threatened by being stared at?
- Have you ever felt like running away?

Follow-up Games
All follow-up games suggested for 82: Security Guard ◆ 83: Agent Game

Adding More Imagination

Statue and Sculpting Games
Games 85–90

Simulation Games
Games 91–92

Social Role-Play Games
Games 93–101

Frozen Pairs

Goals
- Training social and visual perception
- Connecting body language and feelings
- Comparing body language and relationships
- Observing one's feelings

How to Play: Players separate into three small groups. The people in one group are observers. The other two groups move to lively music in the room. When the music stops, they freeze. The observers identify players that are standing opposite or next to each other and have something in common.

Examples
- These two look as if they are having a conversation with each other.
- These two look as if they are separating after a fight.

Variations
- Frozen groups: The observers look at three or more players and look for a "group image" that they might represent.
- One group is the happily dancing group, the other group dances in a sad way. When they freeze, they build interesting pair combinations.

Other possibilities: aggressive and anxious groups, outgoing and shy groups.

Reflections
- In which role did you feel best?
- How did the observers manage seeing pairs?
- Did the dancers adjust to each other's movements?

Follow-up Games
4: Body Language Spells Your Mood ◆ 54: We Are Alike ◆ 86: Sculpting Emotions

Follow-up Games from *101 Life Skills Games for Children*
28: You Sculpt Me ◆ 33–40: Working with You ◆ 66: Freeze Tag ◆ 78: Peace Language ◆ 84–92: Statue and Sculpting Games ◆ 93: Bad News and Good News Pairs ◆ 97–101: Pantomime Play

Sculpting Emotions

Goals
- Sharpening social and emotional perceptions
- Training awareness of emotional body language
- Training visual perception

How to Play: The group splits into three smaller groups. One is the observer group. The other two move to lively music. When the music stops, they freeze. Now the game leader sculpts them by using the "chopping method": He tells the players what emotion the statue should represent, and the players move jerkily (i.e., with choppy movements) into the correct positions.

Examples
- "Transform yourselves into fear statues! Fear! Fear! Fear! Fear! Fear!..." Eventually, everybody is standing in a way that expresses or symbolizes fear.
- "Change into statues of combat ... love ... joy ... longing ... grief!"

Reflections
- In which role did you feel best?
- Did the observers feel the statues expressed themselves well? Which concepts or emotions did the statues express best?
- Did the statue players feel they expressed themselves well? Did they find any concepts or emotions particularly difficult to act out?

Variations
- While the group is moving, a few visitors (i.e., members of the observer group) are outside the room. They are called back in and try to guess what the statues are representing.
- The game leader immediately gives a new assignment: Change into the opposite of what you've just been!

Note: This game illustrates an interesting psychological effect. At first, the players will try to achieve the desired body position by thinking about it—in other words, the mind influences the body. But as soon as the body assumes a certain position, the position itself influences the mind. We can then really feel what our body is expressing, like joy or sadness.

Follow-up Games
85: Frozen Pairs and all of its suggested follow-up games ◆ 87: Statue Groups

87

Statue and Sculpting Games

Statue Groups

Goals
- Sharpening social and emotional perception
- Emotional sensitization
- Learning coordination and cooperation

How to Play: Statues are formed as in Sculpting Emotions (Game #86). The frozen individuals move, following the game leader's instructions, toward each other with the "chopping method" and form small groups of three to six players, representing a concept given by the game leader.

A small observer group helps with the reflection again.

Reflections
- Was it easier to express the desired ideas alone or as a group?
- Which expressions (alone or as a group) had the strongest effect on the observers?

Variations
- After participating in the reflection about the other groups, each group takes a turn trying to recreate their own structure.
- Dream images: Individual observers lie down on the floor. The statues are created around them.

Follow-up Games
All follow-up games suggested for 85: Frozen Pairs ◆ 86: Sculpting Emotions ◆ 88: Family Statues

101 More Life Skills Games for Children **137**

Family Statues

Goals
- Recognizing family roles and family structures
- Acting in different family roles

How to Play: Groups of three to six players are formed who first try to represent the concept of community and then the concept of family by sculpting themselves into a group of statues. The expression of the two ideas will differ in that a concrete distribution of roles will be missing in the representation of community, while in the family, roles such as father, mother, and child may be visible.

Next, each group concentrates on how to portray their own family. They may be taking a family picture, at home doing their own things in the living room, or having a family vacation. The family scene can be one of harmony or conflict. After all the groups have figured out how to create their families, each group "performs" their set of statues while the other groups analyze them. They guess what the players are doing, which player might have assumed which role in the family, and what the situation is. Statements about the family relationships are also made.

Variations
- Who would like to portray her own family?
- Who would like to portray a family of his friends, or from literature or a movie?
- How does a family change when an important incident occurs (death, wedding, pregnancy, illness, graduation, job)?
- The other players are reporters looking for "the family of the week" by doing family interviews for the paper they work for.

Reflections
- What do the terms "functional" and "dysfunctional" mean when applied to a family?
- What are "complete" and "incomplete" families?

- In the families portrayed, which family member can assert herself best? What hierarchies are there in the families? Are there subliminal conflicts? How are decisions made in these families?

Role Plays
- A family member comes to dinner with happy/awkward/sad/monstrous/worrying news.
- One family member has won the lottery. Will the money be shared?

Follow-up Games
40–45: Working with You ◆ 52–59: Cooperation Games ◆ 67–73: Relationship Games ◆ 87: Statue Groups ◆ 89: Statues as Mood Meters ◆ 91–92: Simulation Games

Follow-up Games from *101 Life Skills Games for Children*
28: You Sculpt Me ◆ 45–51: Cooperation Games ◆ 84–92: Statue and Sculpting Games

Statues as Mood Meters

Goals

- Communicating emotions
- Responding to the group's mood

How to Play: The players use their bodies to express how they are feeling.

Examples

- One player feels like running away.
- One player turns away from the group with her hands over her ears.
- One player stands with her arms raised over her head. She feels comfortable in the group.
- One player stretches while sitting in his chair.

Reflections

- What does your body language tell others?
- What would have to change so your body language changes? What would your body then look like?
- Try a new posture for the same feeling!

Variation: The game leader gives imagined situations and the players show with their bodies what they think of them. For example: "Imagine the school is burning!"

Follow-up Games
1–10: What I'm Feeling ◆ 18: Trick or Trait ◆ 22–34: Getting to Know You ◆ 35: Yes No Yes No ◆ 88: Family Statues ◆ 90: Freeze Frame

Follow-up Games from *101 Life Skills Games for Children*
1–5: What I Like ◆ 27–32: Understanding You ◆ 84–92: Statue and Sculpting Games ◆ 97–101: Pantomime Play

Freeze Frame

Goals
- Improving problem relationships within the group
- Understanding personal conflicts

How to Play: This is a game to be used when two or more group members have had a conflict with each other and have been unable to resolve it in any other way. The group leader asks the people to sculpt themselves into statues illustrating the conflict.

Example: One member of the group, Jack, accidentally tripped another member, Jill, during a sports activity. Jill thinks he did it on purpose. Jack now assumes a statue pose to show how he was looking the other way when Jill tripped. Jill assumes a statue pose to show what she was doing when she tripped. The two players hold the pose. If the players disagree about what happened, they can act out two different versions of the event.

Reflections
- Does seeing the conflict clearly help to resolve it?
- How does each group member feel?
- How have the other group members avoided such a conflict?

Note: It's hard not to laugh when you're a statue of yourself! The players should be encouraged to get into the most extreme positions possible to help them see that their conflicts might actually be silly. Use this game to deal with minor misunderstandings only. Only trained therapists can deal with deeper conflicts and conflicts that have arisen outside of the school setting.

Follow-up Games
27: Meet Me Halfway ◆ 45: Accidental Partners ◆ 52–59: Cooperation Games ◆ 67–73: Relationship Games ◆ 76: Playing Politics ◆ 89: Statues as Mood Meters ◆ 93–101: Social Role-Play Games

Follow-up Games from *101 Life Skills Games for Children*
22: Gathering Names ◆ 23: Autograph Book ◆ 50: Tug of War ◆ 58: The Comforter Game ◆ 84–92: Statue and Sculpting Games

New Highway

Props: Written information; pictures and other materials

Goals
- Training cognitive skills
- Tackling projects
- Learning to assert oneself
- Training rhetorical skills
- Learning about roles

How to Play: In this game, players consider a town that is drowning in traffic jams, noise, and pollution. Most residents along Main Street favor the construction of a new highway that would redirect the traffic around the town, but some restaurant owners and business people are against it because they're afraid they'll lose customers. The town is located in an area worthy of preservation, and a group of environmentalists suggests an alternative solution.

The game leader can ask the group to make their own structure and create their own roles for playing the game, or they can use the detailed guidelines for structuring and playing simulation games that are given under "Standard Organization of Simulation Games" on the next page.

Other Examples
- The family's rental agreement will expire in two years. Where to move?
- The mayor would like the school community to participate in remodeling the school.

Reflections
- Who was better informed?
- Which players were eloquent?
- Which players cooperated well so they could assert themselves?
- Who reacted fast and effectively when the game took unexpected turns?

Standard Organization of Simulation Games

In simulation games, players get a description (usually in written form) of a problem or conflict. In addition, each player gets a detailed description of her role. In this description, the person's profession, age, gender, attitudes, and qualities are usually given. The description particularly focuses on the person's attitude toward the given conflict or problem. The role description may also contain sentences that the player can use in the game.

Additional written information, pictures, and other illustrative materials may also be provided. The older the children are, the more detailed the information about the given problem can be before the actual game starts. Ideally, the players also have enough preparation time. The game often doesn't last longer than an hour but, in the case of some projects for fourteen-year-olds, the preparation time can last up to a week. Players who are well informed generally do better in these games.

With younger players it is more appropriate to play an "improvised simulation game" with brief descriptions of the situation and roles. Preparation time focuses largely on verbal exchanges of information and consultations among the players.

Preparation
- Collecting information from flyers, books, or research with public authorities (game leader).
- Collecting arguments from like-minded people.
Example: All business owners, environmentalists, and the mayor meet. They make connections with other town residents, visit them, and exchange opinions. The players tell each other their professions and ages.

Playing the Game
- First Discussion Phase: The mayor invites everyone to a town meeting.
- Consultation phase: Like-minded people adjourn to consult with each other or collect more information.
- Second discussion phase: The discussion is resumed. Various means of manipulation, influencing, or resistance can be employed.
- Assessment: Observers assess the verbal and tactical behavior of the players.

The simulation game is usually played as a discussion game. A family table, a conference room, or a restaurant may serve as the setting.

A jury judges the game when it is over.

Note: Two groups can prepare the simulation game at the same time. Some roles can be played by two people. It is also possible to appoint "free" players who write their own role descriptions. These players can liven up the game by introducing elements of uncertainty or surprise.

Variations

- If there are two groups, they can play the main part of the game one after each other (the other group leaves the room in the meantime or watches as an audience).
- If there are two groups, after the preparation phase one set of players take on the role of observers. Each of them has to observe one player. She can give him tips during the consultation phase. In the game reflection, they report their observations.

Follow-up Games

76: Playing Politics ◆ 92: Reservoir

Reservoir

Props: Printed descriptions of roles

Goals

- Training cognitive skills
- Tackling projects
- Learning to assert oneself
- Training rhetorical skills
- Learning about roles

How to Play: This game is similar to New Highway (Game #91). Please refer to the section "Standard Organization of Simulation Games" on page 154 for information on how to set up and play the game.

Description of Situation:
A brook meanders through a wooded glen that is surrounded by largely un-spoiled woodland, except for a small skiing area that can be reached by a small mountain road. An idyllic mountain lake, the surrounding mountains, and the wildlife park attract tourists. The meadow is sparsely populated. The river water is sweet and the fishing is good. In the summer, the locals visit the sand banks to swim. The river's flow is only disrupted by a few channels or dams. However, according to newspaper reports, there is talk of building a dam and turning the lake into a reservoir. A government agency has commissioned an expert report on water flow, local energy needs, and environmental impact. This is causing much debate among citizens, businesses, nonprofit organizations, and the government. However, no action has been taken yet.

Six players are given specific roles (see below). The other players in the group can be divided into regular citizens, whom the six players try to convince, and "free" players, who write their own role descriptions and create their own roles. Ideally, there should be a balance of people arguing for and against the construction of the dam.

Role Description 1:
Inn owner, resident for 30 years. Her inn is a popular destination. She does not want any changes. When she is contradicted, she easily flares up.

Role Description 2:
Construction worker, 30 years old, father of three, currently unemployed. Not averse to meaningful innovation.

Role Description 3:
Owner of shipping company, 40 years old, single. His business is not doing well at the moment and relies very much on major construction projects. Often stubborn in conversation.

Role Description 4:
Teacher, 25 years old. Doesn't know how long she'll live in this valley as the school might be closed soon due to the small number of children living there. She is considered an environmentalist. In conversation, she tends to lecture.

Role Description 5:
Owner of wildlife park, 60 years old. She is difficult to convince. She frequently has disagreements with authorities about her wildlife park.

Role Description 6:
Mayor, 52 years old. Has a lot of grandchildren that like to go swimming with him in the lake. He is an enthusiastic fisherman. He tries to please all voters. The municipal budget is low.

Additional Information

Statements from the water rights authorities:
"According to a study we commissioned, building a dam would lower the quality of the water beneath the dam by two grades.

"The fishing rights would be transferred to the operating company of the dam, i.e., the power company. Fishing cards would also be issued to tourists at a low rate. The water level under the dam would drop by two thirds. Fish stock would dwindle.

"Cruising the reservoir with rowing or motor boats would be possible with the permission of the power company."

Statement from a high government official:
"Before the elections, an increase of the power supply by water power was promised. The energy demand has increased by 2 percent within one year. We need power stations so the government is commissioning studies of all untapped rivers, including this mountain brook."

Statement from a nature protection club:
"We are against the dam. This is the last largely unexploited valley in this region. Part of the valley is in the nature preserve that the government is planning, and the planned water supply dam would be located right outside of it.

Many protected animals, especially the rare peregrine falcon, have their habitat around the planned water supply dam. A rare lily plant can be found here. We would oppose the construction of the dam with all of our might."

Statements from the tourist agency:
"Arguments for building the dam: The road would be improved and could handle the stream of tourists better. Around the reservoir, recreational resorts as well as swimming and sports centers could be opened. Tourist enterprises could be offered generous loans.

"Arguments against building the dam: Tourists who appreciated the quietness of the place might stay away. Years of construction would reduce the current tourism. Construction workers would not bring in enough business to replace it. But all in all, the income of the tourist enterprises would remain about the same."

Statement from the power company:
"Due to the low water level, the mountain brook would be considered as the location for a small power station only when it becomes absolutely necessary. The site is conceivably unsuitable for a reservoir. The power company would construct it only at great expense. We fear opposition from the people, which would delay construction for years."

Follow-up Games
56: Designing a Classroom ◆ 57: Designing an Apartment ◆ 58: Designing a City ◆ 76: Playing Politics ◆ 91: New Highway

Lip Sync

Goals
- Asserting oneself
- Learning to cooperate

For more information on the goals of social role-play games like Lip Sync, see the Note below.

How to Play: Based on how well they have completed their recent assignments, two players are chosen to make a presentation to the class.

Together, outside the classroom, they plan their presentation. One player will do the talking, and the other will handle the action part and try to move her lips to match what her partner is saying. Then, they swap functions.

Examples
- Radio announcer
- Convenience store cashier
- Teacher

Reflections
- Are you more the talking or the acting type?
- Did this game help you to be patient with your partner?

Follow-up Games
94: Shadow Play ◆ 95: Role Reversal ◆ 96: Interview ◆ 97: Report ◆ 98: Doppelganger ◆ 99: Inside and Outside ◆ 100: Epic Game ◆ 101: Personified Influences

Note on Social Role Plays: Most role plays mentioned in this book are social role plays. They primarily focus on fostering the following five goals:

1. Role distance: the ability to see oneself as separate from the role one is playing.

2. Being able to tolerate various points of view: learning to bear frustration arising from roles, counter roles, and side roles.

3. *Empathy:* being responsive to one's partner in a role play.

4. *Being conscious of the system:* recognizing that one's own behavior can change how the group behaves

5. *Acting in solidarity:* being able to achieve goals by planning and acting together.

In a wider sense, role plays are always social role plays as every game involves social learning. Role plays foster and develop social behavior in the game, give insight into and create social relations, and demonstrate social interrelations. They also show us conflicts and possible solutions, and require both verbal and nonverbal communication. As such, role plays can contribute significantly to mutual understanding and social learning.

Shadow Play

Goal

- Introducing an activity

For more information on the goals of social role-play games, see the Note on page 149.

How to Play: After the basic version of any game has been played, it is played again while a group of onlookers, or "shadows," pantomime what the players are doing. By using their bodies, they can understand better what the players are going through.

Reflection: Which parts of the game did you experience more intensely by using your body in this way?

Follow-up Games

93: Lip Sync and all of its suggested follow-up games

any
size

Role Reversal

Goals
- Dealing with conflict
- Understanding authorities and outsiders
- Dealing with power

For more information on the goals of social role-play games, see the Note on page 149.

How to Play: Players swap roles after improvising a scene from another game. They play the scene again with the roles reversed. In another round, they try to change their behavior completely as they play the different roles.

Examples
- One player has a birthday present for the other, but is too shy to give it to him.
- A bully is trying to take someone's lunch away from her.

Reflections
- Which role did you feel more comfortable with?
- Which person acted correctly, in your opinion?

Follow-up Games
93: Lip Sync and all of its suggested follow-up games

Interview

Goals

- Uncovering motives and backgrounds
- Understanding behavior

For more information on the goals of social role-play games, see the Note on page 149.

How to Play: After a role play is performed (see example below), reporters interview one player.

Example: Let's say the player played a strict father. He would be asked, "What's your method of raising children?" "What bothers you particularly about your son?" "How were you brought up?"

Reflection: What additional information did the partners in the role play gain from the interview? Will this information influence their behavior if they play the scene over again?

Follow-up Games
93: Lip Sync and all of its suggested follow-up games

Report

Props: Tape recorder

Goals
- Analyzing and interpreting behavior

For more information on the goals of social role-play games, see the Note on page 149.

How to Play: One role-play scene is played in pantomime. A "reporter" comments on what is happening in suitable style. Her report can be taped. When the tape is played, the players do the role play again but act according to her report instead.

Note: The game can be played in slow motion so that the reporter's comments can keep up with the action. Alternatively, the reporter can shout, "Freeze!" During these breaks, she can report on what came before.

Reflections
- Has the reporter interpreted the players' acting correctly?
- What types of behavior were more prone to wrong interpretations?

Follow-up Games
93: Lip Sync and all of its suggested follow-up games

Doppelganger

Goals
- Training awareness of others' emotions
- Expressing feelings nonverbally

For more information on the goals of social role-play games, see the Note on page 149.

How to Play: After playing the basic form of a role play, players reenact the scene in silent pantomime. Behind every role player, there is another player who expresses out loud what he thinks are the role player's thoughts.

Reflections
- Why don't all of our true feelings and thoughts come up in a role-play dialog?
- When do we usually suppress our thoughts and feelings?

Follow-up Games
93: Lip Sync and all of its suggested follow-up games

Inside and Outside

Goal
- Making inhibitions visible

For more information on the goals of social role-play games, see the Note on page 149.

How to Play: An observer in the group shouts "Stop!" at a point in a role play when he thinks the player isn't representing her own personal attitude. Then the scene is played again, with the observer taking the role. He plays it up to the point when he had shouted, "Stop!" showing the group how he thought the original player really felt. Now the original player takes over the role again, and the game continues.

Reflections
- What does the original player think of the suggested variation?
- In a second round, would she prefer to play it the way she had originally played it, or the way the observer played it?

Follow-up Games
93: Lip Sync and all of its suggested follow-up games

Epic Game

Goal
- Trying out alternative ways of acting

For more information on the goals of social role-play games, see the Note on page 149.

How to Play: After playing the basic form of a role play, a person who did not play takes over as game leader. She narrates the plot in a form that she likes, changing details. After a few sentences, she says, "Go!" signaling to the role players to play the contents of the story narrated so far. When the game leader calls out "Stop!" the game is interrupted, and she continues telling the story.

Note: Other alternatives can be offered by introducing additional game leaders.

Reflection: Which version of the plot felt the most "right" to the players?

Follow-up Games
93: Lip Sync and all of its suggested follow-up games

Personified Influences

Goal
- Discovering how personal wishes do not always coincide with social norms

For more information on the goals of social role-play games, see the Note on page 149.

How to Play: After playing the basic form of a role play, the group reflects about social norms that were fulfilled by the people in the game but which were contrary to the preferences of these people. Which norm is in conflict with what need here?

Example: The weather is beautiful! Peter's friends are in front of his house encouraging him to join them in a game of soccer. He tells them he has to study today. For a while after that, his friends don't come to pick him up any more. In this example, the sense of duty and the desire to play are in conflict with each other.

Two external observers now play a dispute between Mister Duty and Miss Play.

Reflections
- Which of the two people had the stronger arguments?
- Do strong arguments always win?

Follow-up Games
93: Lip Sync and all of its suggested follow-up games

Keyword Index

The Games Arranged
by Specific Categories

Advanced Games

8: Mood Music
10: Mood Dice
12: Finish My Thought
17: The "I" Museum
18: Trick or Trait
20: Pieces of Personality
21: Help Wanted
23: What's My Name?
27: Meet Me Halfway
28: Two-Way Interview
29: Disposable Secrets
31: Rumor Factory
35: Yes No Yes No
38: 20 Questions
42: We're on the Same Page
44: Two Writers, One Story
45: Accidental Partners
51: The Goofy Game
54: We Are Alike
55: Birthday Present
56: Designing a Classroom
57: Designing an Apartment
58: Designing a City
59: Space Expedition
61: The Blind Person and the Movie
62: Blindness in Everyday Life
63: The Blind Group
64: Blind Pool
65: Hearing Nothing
66: Disability of the Extremities
69: My Place in the Group
70: Spider Web
75: President of Praise
76: Playing Politics
77: Circle of Threat
79: War Dance

80: Face-off
82: Security Guard
83: Agent Game
87: Statue Groups
88: Family Statues
91: New Highway
92: Reservoir
93: Lip Sync
94: Shadow Play
95: Role Reversal
96: Interview
97: Report
98: Doppelganger
99: Inside and Outside
100: Epic Game
101: Personified Influences

Games Requiring a Large Space

48: Lost in the Dark Woods
49: Stumbling over Roots
50: Through the Thicket
84: Chase

Games Not Requiring Props

2: Flashlight
4: Body Language Spells Your Mood
14: Who Said That?
22: The Story of My Name
23: What's My Name?
29: Disposable Secrets
31: Rumor Factory
33: Favorite Place
39: Two Peas in a Pod
47: Name Chain
48: Lost in the Dark Woods
49: Stumbling over Roots

Games Requiring Physical Contact

Games Requiring Musical Accompaniment

SmartFun *activity books encourage imagination, social interaction, and self-expression in children. Games are organized by the skills they develop, and simple icons indicate appropriate age levels, times of play, and group size. Most games are noncompetitive and require no special training. The series is widely used in schools, homes, and summer camps.*

101 RELAXATION GAMES FOR CHILDREN: Finding a Little Peace and Quiet In Between *by* Allison Bartl

The perfect antidote for unfocused and fidgety young children, these games help to maintain or restore order, refocus children's attention, and break up classroom routine. Most games are short and can be used as refreshers or treats. They lower noise levels in the classroom and help to make learning fun. **Ages 6 and up.**

>> 128 pages ... 96 illus. ... Paperback $14.95 ... Spiral bound $19.95

101 PEP-UP GAMES FOR CHILDREN: Refreshing, Recharging, Refocusing *by* Allison Bartl

Children get re-energized with these games! Designed for groups of mixed-age kids, the games require little or no preparation or props, with easier games toward the beginning and more advanced ones toward the end. All games are designed to help children release pent-up energy by getting them moving. **Ages 6–10.**

>> 128 pages ... 86 illus. ... Paperback $14.95 ... Spiral bound $19.95

101 QUICK-THINKING GAMES + RIDDLES FOR CHILDREN
by Allison Bartl

The 101 games and 65 riddles in this book will engage and delight students and bring fun into the classroom. All the games, puzzles, and riddles work with numbers and words, logic and reasoning, concentration and memory. Children use their thinking and math and verbal skills while they sing, clap, race, and read aloud. Certain games also allow kids to share their knowledge of songs, fairytales, and famous people. **Ages 6–10.**

>> 144 pages ... 95 illus. ... Paperback $14.95 ... Spiral bound $19.95

101 LANGUAGE GAMES FOR CHILDREN: Fun and Learning with Words, Stories and Poems
by Paul Rooyackers

Language is perhaps the most important human skill, and play can make language more creative and memorable. The games in this book have been tested in classrooms around the world. They range from letter games to word play, story-writing, and poetry games, including Hidden Word and Haiku Arguments. **Ages 4 and up.**

>> 144 pages ... 27 illus. ... Paperback $14.95 ... Spiral bound $19.95

101 MUSIC GAMES FOR CHILDREN: Fun and Learning with Rhythm and Song by Jerry Storms

All you need to play these games are music CDs and simple instruments, many of which kids can make from common household items. Many games are good for large group settings, such as birthday parties, others are easily adapted to classroom needs. No musical knowledge is required. **Ages 4 and up.**

>> 160 pages ... 30 illus. ... Paperback $14.95 ... Spiral bound $19.95

101 DANCE GAMES FOR CHILDREN: Fun and Creativity with Movement by Paul Rooyackers

These games encourage children to interact and express how they feel in creative ways, without words. They include meeting and greeting games, cooperation games, story dances, party dances, "musical puzzles," dances with props, and more. No dance training or athletic skills are required. **Ages 4 and up.**

>> 160 pages ... 36 illus. ... Paperback $14.95 ... Spiral bound $19.95

101 DRAMA GAMES FOR CHILDREN: Fun and Learning with Acting and Make-Believe by Paul Rooyackers

Drama games are a fun, dynamic form of play that help children explore their imagination and creativity. These noncompetitive games include introduction games, sensory games, pantomime games, story games, sound games, games with masks, games with costumes, and more. The "play-ful" ideas help to develop self-esteem, improvisation, communication, and trust. **Ages 4 and up.**

>> 160 pages ... 30 illus. ... Paperback $14.95 ... Spiral bound $19.95

101 IMPROV GAMES FOR CHILDREN ... by Bob Bedore

Improv comedy has become very popular, and this book offers the next step in drama and play: a guide to creating something out of nothing, reaching people using talents you didn't know you possessed. Contains exercises for teaching improv to children, advanced improv techniques, and tips for thinking on your feet — all from an acknowledged master of improv. **Ages 5 and up.**

>> 192 pages ... 65 b/w photos ... Paperback $14.95 ... Spiral bound $19.95

THE YOGA ADVENTURE FOR CHILDREN: Playing, Dancing, Moving, Breathing, Relaxing by Helen Purperhart

Offers an opportunity for the whole family to laugh, play, and have fun together. This book for children 4–12 years old explains yoga stretches and postures as well as the philosophy behind yoga. The exercises are good for a child's mental and physical development, and also improve concentration and self-esteem. **Ages 4–12.**

>> 144 pages ... 75 illus. ... Paperback $14.95 ... Spiral bound $19.95

Printed in the USA
CPSIA information can be obtained
at www.ICGtesting.com
JSHW082208140824
68134JS00014B/506